Travel Light, Move Fast

Travel Light,

Move Fast

ALEXANDRA FULLER

Penguin Press • New York • 2019

PENGUIN PRESS
An imprint of Penguin Random House LLC
penguinrandomhouse.com

"A Long Lifetime" from *Sky Sea Birds Trees Earth House Beasts Flowers*
by Kenneth Rexroth. Published by Unicorn Press, 1971.
Reprinted by permission of the publisher.

LIBRARY OF CONGRESS CATALOGING-IN-PUBLICATION DATA

Names: Fuller, Alexandra, 1969– author.
Title: Travel light, move fast / Alexandra Fuller.
Description: New York : Penguin Press, 2019.
Identifiers: LCCN 2019000116 (print) | LCCN 2019007233 (ebook) |
ISBN 9780698406643 (ebook) | ISBN 9781594206740 (hardcover) |
ISBN 9781984879219 (export)
Subjects: LCSH: Fuller, Alexandra, 1969– —Family. |
Fuller, Tim (Timothy Donald), 1940–2015. | English–Africa—Biography.
Classification: LCC PS3606.U49 (ebook) | LCC PS3606.U49 Z75 2019 (print) |
DDC 813/.6 [B]—dc23
LC record available at https://lccn.loc.gov/2019000116

Printed in the United States of America
1   3   5   7   9   10   8   6   4   2

Book design by Daniel Lagin

Penguin is committed to publishing works of quality and integrity.
In that spirit, we are proud to offer this book to our readers; however,
the story, the experiences, and the words are the author's alone.

For my infinitely courageous three

Sarah, Fi, and Cecily

With Infinite Love

Young and Old

When all the world is young, lad,
And all the trees are green;
And every goose a swan, lad,
And every lass a queen;
Then hey for boot and horse, lad,
And round the world away!
Young blood must have its course, lad,
And every dog his day.

—CHARLES KINGSLEY,
SONG FROM *THE WATER BABIES*

Contents

PART TWO
A Widow's Farm, Chirundu, Zambia

Travel Light, Move Fast

PART ONE

A Very Good Death

Budapest, Hungary

A Long Lifetime

A long lifetime
Peoples and places
And the crisis of mankind—
What survives is the crystal—
Infinitely small—
Infinitely large—

—KENNETH REXROTH

CHAPTER ONE

In the Unlikely Event of Money,
Buy Two Tickets to Paris

O h, hello, Bobo," Dad said, waking up from an induced coma to find me by his bedside. He looked around as best he could. "Bus station?" he asked.

"Budapest," I said.

"Oh?" Dad said, fretting the lines and tubes that ran to his mouth and into his nose and into needles that disappeared under his skin where the Zambian sun had scalded an indelible brown line across his neck. The veins on his hands stood out, a worker's hands, muscled and thick; there were needles slipped in there too.

"The poor man's Paris," I explained, cupping his hands in mine, the way you catch a large moth, gingerly.

"Ah," Dad said, relaxing a bit.

Dad loved Paris in the spring; he loved Paris, the whole song. Something had happened to him there the year he left high school; love perhaps, or his first taste of freedom from the boiled-cabbage, gin-wrecked gloom of his British upbringing. After that, for the rest of his life, every time he came into extra money, which wasn't often, he'd threaten to buy two tickets to Paris.

"Those Frogs know how it's done. Start with champagne, end with absinthe; bring your dog to supper and no one gives a *merde* if you get off with the waiter," he said.

Dad took my mother to Paris three times; he'd taken me once. He tried to get my sister to go for her fortieth birthday, but Vanessa had just delivered her sixth child and had endured a subsequently exhausting recovery in a noisy Lusaka clinic and she wasn't in the mood to race our father to the top of the Eiffel Tower, or to savor new-in-season blackberries with a bottle of plonk on the Île de la Cité.

"If I show up with two tickets to Paris, will you come with me?" Dad had always asked the Scottish nurse with the cobalt-blue eyes who'd been our neighbor in southern Africa, back in the days my parents tried their hand at farming in a war zone. Auntie Rena, Vanessa and I had called her; in a war, you feel related to everyone, trauma bonded.

"Why yes, Tim," Auntie Rena had always replied.

DAD HATED HOSPITALS. "They won't let you smoke, you can't get a drink when you really need one, and they always want to poke you in places not designed for poking." He hated doctors too, on account of their propensity to attract dying or wounded people. "Then finish off the job."

He'd only been in a hospital one other time, back in the seventies, after he'd run himself over while fixing the brakes on a car, also during our farming-in-a-war-zone phase. The workshop, built by the previous owner of the farm, a melancholy alcoholic, wasn't level. "Should be good drainage, though," Dad said, looking on the bright side of the noticeably tilted pounded-dirt floor. "If there's a flood."

But this was revolutionary-era Rhodesia—as it was back then, unpredictable, upended, brilliant—and our farm was in a rain shadow, so although we had floods, mostly we had drought, and it was a heavy, mine-proofed station wagon that had slowly rolled over Dad while the workshop staff looked on in impotent horror.

"Poor Dad," Mum had said. "Squashed flat as a cockroach and still he kept insisting there was nothing wrong with him that couldn't be fixed with an aspirin and a couple of brandies."

Everyone hit panic stations; rare in Rhodesia, it went against our professed national character. We were the *manliest* of people. "Your father was the first person to be medevaced to town from the valley," Mum said, her nose twitching wistfully. "Until then, people just had to bite the bullet; and in very serious cases, we were rattled into the hospital in a mine-proof Land Rover. No shock absorbers to speak of."

It was as if she were explaining to me a sepia-colored version of a life she'd known well, a life that included my father, but which I could barely grasp, as if I'd been nowhere near the actual bright, bloody intensity of it all myself.

"Absolute agony for the victim," Mum said.

"I remember," I said.

"But not," Mum continued, "your father. Paul Dickenson, bless him, drove Dad in his *Mercedes-Benz*"—there was a pause, so I'd have the opportunity to appreciate the full extent of what Mum had just said—"to Brian Van Buren's airstrip and Brian flew him straight to the airfield in Umtali over *enemy* lines."

Things were beginning to blur a little in Mum's narrative, I could tell, *Out of Africa* merging with one of those dashing Second World War movies she loves. But in our real life, in our little Rhodesian Bush War, there really were no enemy lines, no helpful German accents; God and restraint were long gone. There was only the country left; the soil, I mean, and blood.

And the three warring factions: white settlers scattered fatly here, there, everywhere; the Mashona kraaled in the northern two-thirds of the country, the Matabele in the south.

To the death, we white settlers vowed. Naturally, the Mashona and Matabele had no choice but to make the same vow. Even a small child could tell it was going to be a long war, a rotten mess.

The black insurgents had the open support of North Korea, China, and Bono; they were tougher than it's possible to imagine, enduring and patient. They'd been here forever and a generation. Some of those musoja must have been poets, dancers, farmers; war must have been harder for them to wage. Still, the ancestors were with them.

The white Rhodesians had the support of the United States, Israel, South Africa, and the UK; they were well trained, well armed, and ruthless. Most of their army was made up of paid black locals bossed about by white conscripts. A whole country of soldiers, but some of those conscripts must also have been poets, dancers, monks; ruthlessness must have been harder for them to perform. They were ancestor-abandoned and -abandoning.

Dad was assigned to a local unit on the eastern front, which wasn't difficult to find, we were standing on it, but it wasn't easy once he got there. He fought six months of every year with a handful of other white men, neighboring farmers, brothers in arms. They were supposed to stop insurgents coming from Mozambique into Rhodesia. Dad didn't talk about it much; unless in his sleep.

Mum didn't need to be told; she volunteered. She pledged to dig in as if we were seven generations into the place, as if we had actual skin in the game. She gamely donned the uniform, a horrible boxy dress in heavy polyester that would have been better suited to the Bavarian Alps, say, than to the sweltering valleys of eastern Rhodesia.

"Well, obviously we didn't think the war would go on for so long, or that we'd lose," Mum said afterward. She glared at me. "It was a shock when Robert Mugabe got in; I knew exactly what that meant. Or perhaps you don't remember."

I do remember.

Also what happened next, I remembered that too, although it's not just one story, it's thousands of stories, millions maybe. And it's not just our story, or we're in the story, but it didn't happen only to us; it happened to other people too, and we happened upon it in equal measure. In unequal measure, I should say. It'd be generations before the shock waves left the land.

Or it is generations; we're still there.

"So, of course, we stuck it out," Mum concluded.

OURS WAS A NATION in a state at war with itself, no doubt; bodies piled up. We all had family on the front, unless they'd already been taken out, as we said, scribbled, donnered. But the Scripture Union teacher at our junior school reassured us that the blacks had whatever they gave coming back to them. "The sins of the father will be visited onto their children, even unto their children's children," she said.

Meantime, there were army camps and minefields. There were suburbs behind razor wire, dogs patrolling clipped lawns. There were convoys, curfews, sanctions, and censorship. The whole country had been turned into one vast, confusing battlefield and there was no getting off it.

"Oh, Bobo," Mum says. "You do exaggerate."

Mum prefers not to remember the war, or anything about our lives, the way I do. All her stories have the clicking-celluloid and worn-velvet comfort of an old cinema. As a result, her stories are better than mine, more vividly imagined, less depressing.

"And from the airfield," Mum continued brightly, "Dad was taken straight to Umtali General in an ambulance. Imagine! He yelled and yelled. He wanted to be taken to the Wise Owl, the Impala Arms, the Cecil Hotel, anywhere but the hospital. I had to hear all about it from the stretcher-bearers afterward." Mum paused. "Not that it would have made any difference. The driver couldn't hear Dad's desperate entreaties above the wail of the sirens. Oh, those were the good old days, Bobo. There was always something exciting going on."

LIKE LOVE, war's a bloody mess when it's happening, and a worse mess when it's over; but with any distance, you can look back at either and see only the glory, or only the pain. The dusk-obscured truth—somewhere in the middle of all our human messiness—is very difficult to recognize. Honestly, it's so faint through the dim pewter gloaming; it may not even be there at all, shapeless and formless.

Perhaps it's God, or time, or all things; it's grace in any case. Some soldiers claim to have seen it through gun smoke; women pushing life into the world might catch a glimpse of it; it's in the start of everything and in everyone's end, surely. But to have clarity in the routine of your ordinary life, not at the very end, or in extremis: That's amazing grace; and you don't just wake up there either.

There's always a terrible waiting period, a purgatory of doubt, between the suffering and the grace. That's the lonely alone work, weathering the places in between, and dismantling oneself piece by piece meantime, shredding all that can be shredded, returning to dust all that can be eroded. Amazing grace appears when all faith has fled; when final exhaustion has set in; when there're no trails to follow and one carries on anyway.

"Travel light," my father always said. "Move fast."

He followed that advice, practiced what he preached, like it was a key tenet of his personal religion. "When you're all the way down to the bone," he'd told me once, "tobacco, tea, and a mosquito net; that's all you need."

When you're all the way down to the bone.

Dad greatly admired a good sufferer; he remarked on it. Rural southern Africans came in for his highest praise. "Five hundred years of practice, poor bastards," Dad said. The Brits were useless, in his estimation, except the queen. "She can take it on the chin all right." The Italians were undignified. "They cry for their mothers," Dad said. And it was hard to tell with Americans, "because it's all a bit loud."

THE ANNEX OF THE MEN'S WARD of the Umtali General Hospital, where Dad was taken to recover from running himself over, was a new, low-slung barracks hastily erected to accommodate war casualties flooding in from the officially recognized eastern front. "Well, that was literally our kitchen door," Mum explained with studied humility. "It was us, Bobo, and beyond that, it was them."

Injured soldiers sat outside in the sun, or slowly walked about, the ones who could, mouths frozen in a perpetual "oh," as if the vehement amazement of whatever blast had brought them here was still working its way out of their bodies. "Stop gawking," Vanessa reminded me.

The sadness and waste and wrongness of war take decades to work their way out of a place and a people. My father shouted and hurled things in his sleep until the very end. "There're no handles on any of the wardrobes," Mum complained. "And I can't get any of the drawers to open, or close, properly. Dad's shell shock has made toothpicks of the bedroom furniture."

She didn't begrudge the war though; neither did Dad, not really. For them it was what it was; their regrets quite different from mine, less painful probably, our guilt not at all similar. "I felt awkward as hell in that hospital bed. Not that my marksmanship ever caused any gook a sleepless night," Dad said. "But you don't want some other chap to have to bat your innings just because you were bloody fool enough to run yourself over."

So even then, even with his right knee swollen like a watermelon, his right shoulder crushed to a wafer, his ribs cracked, organs bruised, my father had railed against his hospitalization. To ease the strain, Mum smuggled gallons of brandy into the ward, strapped to her body under a kaftan. "The midseventies kaftan. Not very flattering, but *very* practical," Mum said.

Shortly thereafter, Dad organized an impromptu sports day for the shell-shocked amputees: three-legged races, wheelchair jockeying, one-armed cricket. There was a lot of hilarity, but also further accidents and injuries. The sack race was an unmitigated disaster for the hospital's pillowcases.

"He was the worst patient in the history of the Umtali General Hospital," Mum said, with no small degree of fake pride, the way she modestly celebrates when one of her dogs bites someone. "And that's up against some pretty stiff competition, I should think. In the end, they were forced to release him early."

I COULD TELL DAD HAD BEEN a rotten patient in Budapest too. There were saucer-sized bruises up and down his forearms from the restraints they'd had to put on; I'd taken those off right away. He'd tried to escape more than once; and he'd threatened to punch the nurse attempting to give him an enema.

"My husband is very old-fashioned," my mother explained slowly and carefully to the offended nurse, a younger member of staff with regrettably proficient English.

"A beach," the young nurse protested; she had a lot of jewelry on her face, a stud in her tongue flashed. "He called me a beach, and also some other very bad words. Very, very bad."

"Yes, well," Mum said, staring pointedly at one of the nurse's nose piercings. "An Englishman's bottom is his castle."

The young nurse looked astonished, "He's an Englishman?"

I could understand her skepticism.

Dad didn't look like a typical, elderly, dying Englishman, pale and soft, untouched by an excess of ultraviolet light. Fifty years of sunburn, fifty years of tearing the ring out of it. He looked exactly what he was, a banana farmer from Zambia's Zambezi Valley. Any moment, it seemed inevitable he'd sit up, swing his legs over the side of the bed, and say, "Right, no more silly buggers!"

In fact, three weeks earlier, Dad had been on the farm in Zambia with his big, black, gentlemanly mutt, Harry, by his side, delivering a lecture to Comrade Connie, the banana plantation forewoman, on the importance of weeding the bananas and telling her, "Comrade Connie, weeding is next to godliness."

And that's how he should have died. Cracking a joke with Comrade Connie. Dead before he hit the ground, and Comrade Connie would've been there, so would have Harry, to comfort him in those final moments. They'd have called Mr. Chrissford and Mrs. Tembo; Mum would have been summoned.

They'd have had him in the ground by morning, in that heat.

That had been his plan. "A heart attack on the job, or a decent dose of malaria," he'd once told an inquisitive financial adviser when she'd asked about his strategies for retirement; he was in his late sixties at the time. "And until then," he'd added, "I intend to misspend what's left of my youth."

But with bushy-top disease sweeping banana plantations worldwide, yields hadn't quite been up to two tickets to Paris. Two tickets to the poor man's Paris then, and Mum had been having so much fun—swanking about on a riverboat up the Danube, taking in the medieval castles, showing off her very good legs in the famous aquamarine public thermal baths—that he hadn't wanted to mention he didn't feel very well.

"Typical. He didn't complain at all," Mum said. "Then all of a sudden, he said, 'Watch out for that waiter, he's a spy,' and collapsed."

"The waiter's a spy?" I asked.

"Well, he probably was a spy. That's not the point. The point is, Dad suddenly crumpled like a soufflé and I had to call a Hungarian ambulance. Or the spy had to call a Hungarian ambulance."

"You mean the waiter," I said.

"Oh, Bobo," Mum said; disappointed reproach isn't an easy note to strike when the basic emotion is justified irritation. "It's not as simple as it looks, trying to have an emergency in a foreign language."

IN THE END, it took Dad twelve days to die in Budapest.

"Technically, just Pest," Mum said. "Buda's across the river, the hilly pretty part. You never saw it."

Twelve days seems no time, to have it back. But to do it once, alone in a strange city, it was real time and no time, as if it were just he and I suspended in another realm, a holding dock or a leaving station; nowhere we'd ever been before and nowhere from which we'd ever be returning.

Mum was fond of quoting Leslie Poles Hartley, "The past is a foreign country," but I was finding out, so was dying. Or dying was a baffling amalgamation of all countries; the suddenly brief past meeting an endless future in which every breath was now, exactly as they instruct you, the only thing that counted.

I phoned my sister in Zambia as soon I was back in my own room. Mum and I had become such a cause célèbre—we inadvertent longtime guests—the hotel had generously given me a room down the hall from Mum's at no extra cost. The whole staff knew us by name—Madam Fuller and Daughter Fuller—and by tragedy, like we were folklore come to life. They bestowed us sympathetic looks when they passed us in the corridors; we'd receive extra sachets of tea, little cartons of milk. "Such a humane people," Mum had said, her eyes moistening. "It's not how you imagine the Hungarians, is it?"

It wasn't, although truthfully until now I hadn't really taken the time to imagine the Hungarians at all.

"Van?" I was shouting into the phone now. I always shout when I call Zambia, as if the world is what it was, jerky old phone lines under the sea.

Vanessa lives a couple of hours from our parents' farm; they're close neighbors by our standards. I get all my news from home via Vanessa, unless she isn't talking to me, or to Mum and Dad, in which case I get no news, or I get the news as edited by Mum, which requires much insider knowledge, and the ability to listen between the lines.

Predictably, Vanessa and I had reacted very differently to the news of Dad's collapse. I'm fight and flight; I'd immediately set about getting myself from the United States to Budapest. Vanessa's freeze; she'd taken to her bed in the hills above the Kafue River, turned the air-conditioning to North England in winter, and piled a heap of cats on her knees for warmth.

"Oh, huzzit, Al-Bo," Vanessa said. I heard her scuffling about, organizing cats. "I'll just take the phone outside so I don't bug Rich." Rich was Van's husband; we were all scared of bugging him. I pictured Van stuffing one of the Persians under her arm, grabbing her cigarettes, her lighter, looking around for her phone before realizing she was holding it. "Oh, Al, how do we do this? Thank goodness you're there. I don't have what it takes. I'm drained. Bindi says I'm drained."

Bindi was Vanessa's therapist.

Mum drags the word out, the-rapist.

Mum has a powerful dislike for Bindi, especially after Bindi had strongly encouraged Vanessa to complete a twenty-eight-day stint at a clinic in KwaZulu-Natal. Vanessa had done so, and had come back to Zambia with a diagnosis.

"A what?" Mum had asked, but it was too late by then. Vanessa was already in recovery. "She's where?" Mum couldn't bring her self to say the phrase. Bindi had also been recommending for some time now that Vanessa take a break from us, her family. "A mental-health sabbatical?" Mum had repeated, offended, you could tell, by each and every word of the therapist's suggestion. "From us? I've never heard such rot."

In the end, it had been more restful for Vanessa to pretend Bindi hadn't said anything; it had been more peaceful to stay in the eye of the storm than battle through a cyclone to calm. In any case, Vanessa and I were accustomed to drama, acclimated to it, adapted to thrive in its peculiar conditions; drama had always been our family's independent weather system.

"I'm praying for you nonstop," Vanessa said now.

"Thanks," I said.

She sent me inspirational quotes off the internet to keep me going, photos of the hands of God poking through the clouds. She said she'd set up a table for Dad on her veranda overlooking the hills and the little game farm where drongos swooped above the long grass. She'd have Mr. Nixon bring him endless trays of tea. Mr. Nixon is the cook at the Rock.

The Rock is Vanessa and Rich's house. It's built on prime snake habitat. Vanessa has a lot of dogs and cats, though, and they tend to alert her when there are snakes, but also when there aren't, frankly. It's all very chaotic, but the staff is excellent; they sweep around in their pressed uniforms and keep the place looking orderly.

"I don't know how they do it," Mum always says. She leaves surreptitious extravagant tips for the staff; Rich doesn't like it. He likes total control at all times of all things.

Mr. Nixon has worked for Rich for so long, the two have become mirror images of each other. Mr. Nixon has the figure and grace of an Edgar Degas ballerina. Rich does not. We call Rich "God" to his face. Or really, to his knees; he commands a room. Mr. Nixon, on the other hand, leaves a room backward, one limb at a time, like he's just received a knighthood; I don't know how he keeps it up day after day, the irony, I mean. "Mr. Nixon doesn't like me, but he'll do anything for Dad," Vanessa said.

Mum wasn't much use either. She is terrific in a crisis, but in the non-emergency of dying, she was aimless. She drifted about the weedy hospital grounds, where patients from the oncology ward perched on benches among parched weeds, smoking. Hungarian ambulances—yellow and green like grocery delivery vans—

pulled up from time to time with crashed, collapsed bodies that then had to be wrestled upstairs; the elevator hadn't worked in months.

A couple of dozen stray cats streamed through the undergrowth or curled up in patches of tattered shade; Mum named them all, had long conversations with the gateman about their breeding. As if stray cats have breeding. "Of course they do," Mum said.

Of course they did: *Felis silvestris*, Mum informed me; some of them were a European wildcat hybrid, explaining, she said, their gorgeous stripes. It was a problem for the integrity of the species, this crossbreeding with domestic strays. She'd learned all this from the gateman, he with almost no English, Mum never having tried until now a single word of Hungarian.

At mealtimes, Mum ferried down Dad's untouched trays of food—beige- and concrete-colored pastes and porridges—and spread them around the grounds for the cats.

"Smoking's a national pastime," she observed. "They must get them started as infants. Budapest's freshest air is like being in an English pub fifty years ago."

That, and the heat wave, the pollution, the stress, Mum's allergy to cats, her asthma, of course she got hopelessly sick too; her lungs weak anyway after all those years of everyone's secondhand smoke. She was wracked with frequent coughing fits. She was losing weight.

"No, no, Bobo. I'm fine," Mum insisted.

But I carted her back to the hotel nevertheless. It would be just like me to rush over to help one parent die, and accidentally kill the other. I tuned the television to a nice, soothing village murder, a BBC production; all the proper accents in all the proper places. I mixed Mum a drink and ordered her to stay in bed.

"See if you can figure out whodunit before the end," I said.

"The cats," Mum protested. "Who will feed the cats? Will you feed the cats?"

She slumped, suddenly tiny on the too-big hotel bed. Her eyes slid over the fluffed, stacked pillows to the novel still sitting on Dad's bedside table, an Ian Fleming. "At least he went out with a good James Bond," Mum said. "You wouldn't want the last book you read to be absolute drivel, would you?"

My heart seized with helplessness.

I knew her stress wasn't just Dad dying, it was also being separated from her library and her pets and from her life on the little fish and banana farm in the hot, drought-prone valley where my parents had finally settled after decades of nearly itinerant drifting around southern and south-central Africa.

She missed the little mopane forest in the clay pan at the top of the farm, the fishponds overseen by silver-pink barked baobab trees, the tangle of wild between the farmyard and the banana plantation, the wide Zambezi River swirling brown and lazy, flowing ever south toward Mozambique.

If not for the snakes, buffalo bean, and other perils, Mum could walk the farm's boundary with eyes closed, past the seasonal wetland on the farm's easternmost boundary, through the river in which a cow-eating crocodile lived during the rains, then up the hill toward the fishponds, and from there westerly home along the swath cut through the bush for the electricity lines.

I knew my mother knew all those paths like a mantra; they were a sacred refrain to her. She needed her routine of a twice-daily walk with her flock of ill-behaved dogs; her evening consultation with Professor, her erudite ginger cat. She required the constant companionship of wild birds, skinks, monkeys, and snakes. The shouting of hippos from the river comforted her.

"Don't worry," I told her. "I'll feed the cats."

SO IN THE MORNINGS when I arrived, and in the evenings before I left, I fed the cats and took photos on my phone to prove it to Mum, heads down, tails emerging like little question marks from the contented clowder. The rest of the time I sat by Dad's bedside and sweated in the late-summer heat and waited.

It was weirdly familiar, like being back in boarding school, a perpetual season of sweltering humidity. Except this time our terms overlapped, Dad's and mine, meted out hour by hour together, the end of his term signaling the end of mine. It felt of longing and displacement both; and because of that, camaraderie. Also, like boarding school, there was the capricious nature of a large authoritative institution with which to contend.

For example, as the result of a sudden new rule—a rule that appeared to coincide with some loudly expressed views I had regarding my father's care—visiting hours were severely curtailed. Now visitors were allowed in for only half an hour morning and evening; the doors to the ICU were suddenly locked during the day.

I pretended not to notice.

A couple of times, the young nurse with the regrettably proficient English ordered me out of the ward, but inspired by a technique I'd watched Vanessa perfect for most of our childhoods I made vague, agreeable noises and smiled as angelically as possible. But I didn't leave my post.

Jazmin, I discovered, was her name.

"Very common," Mum said, when I divulged this piece of information as part of our evening routine, a debriefing of all that had happened at the hospital that day. Mum especially relished news of the escalating tensions between Jazmin and me, usually taking the side of the nurse.

"Jazmin," Mum said, trying out the name again. "Well, no wonder." Mum attempted a humble expression. "I named you after a princess. Alexandra, the Honorable Lady Ogilvy. Minor royalty, but not nobody."

Jazmin had printed out copies of the new visiting hours in English, and taped them not only at the entrance to the ICU but also, aggressively I felt, on the wall next to Dad's bed. "Quite right," Mum said, reverting to the nurse's side. "Patients need their rest, and nurses need to do their work."

Still, I persisted.

"Don't bother Dad too long," Mum reminded me as I left her every morning, alone at our breakfast table for two, a tiny fake daisy in a little white pot. Mum eked out her time over tea, forcing herself to eat two or three pastries with lots of extra butter to keep up her strength. "Dad does not like lots of disturbance," she said pointedly. "At least not lots of disturbance that he doesn't generate himself."

But I stayed all day.

I'm such a reluctant rebel. I'm a rule keeper, in fact. I imagined Jazmin's angry eyes on me, I imagined she'd spread her poison; I imagined everyone wanted me out. I wondered how Vanessa had kept it up her whole life, her utter indifference to authority; it's impressively harder than it looks to pull off.

BEYOND THE HOSPITAL WALLS, the city sweltered and stalled. Hundreds of thousands of refugees on the border had been pressing relentlessly west all summer, now they were here in central Hungary on the outskirts of the city; authorities had closed the central train station.

Meantime, Dad froze under the blankets, hypothermic as his

organs closed down. Then he turned a contradictory healthy shade of pink and began to sweat a little. "I've been very lucky," Dad said suddenly, on the eleventh day.

I'd been sitting very still on the metal chair I'd pulled up next to the bed, listening to Dad's labored breaths, watching his chest rise and fall, wondering if he'd slipped into something deeper than sleep. Behind me, a couple of nurses drank coffee and chatted in front of vintage computers.

I squeezed Dad's arm. "Dad?"

"I've been very lucky," Dad said again; as if, even dying, he wanted to point out that there were fates far worse than his; and even then, there were more or less fortunate ways to die.

"IT'S POSSIBLE HE'S SAID his last words," I warned Mum. I brought her to visiting hours that evening; the sun still building on the heat of the day.

"Did he mention me?" she asked.

"Of course," I said.

"Who else?" Mum wanted to know.

He'd mentioned Mr. Kalusha, the farm's driver; and Mr. Chrissford, the farm's foreman; and Mrs. Hilda Tembo, the farmhouse's cook; and Boss Shupi, the barman at the pub at the bottom of the farm. "He mentioned Harry a lot too," I said.

"Quite right," Mum said approvingly.

Dad's corner of the ICU had taken on the scent of the farm: diesel, soil, fever trees, bananas, the roiling Zambezi River. The essence of that soil and water were eking out of him now, the room was taking on my father's life; it was a clear exchange.

"He still looks good, though," Mum said. "Doesn't he?" And he did; slightly flushed, breathing with concentrated effort as if participating in something slightly more active than dying; like he was comfortably cycling up a gentle incline. He'd never have done that in real life, or yoga, but that was his breath.

Mum and I sat on either side of the bed and watched Dad for a while; the effort he was making. "Oh, Bobo," Mum whispered. "It's the final stretch, isn't it?"

"I think so," I whispered.

Time was suddenly revealed to be utterly surreal, an impossibly demanding reality; there's no turning back the clock; there's no way to shove the minutes behind you, or to drag out an end. Everything is always starting and ending all the time, without cease. It was only the stories we told that gave time the impression of shape, or meaning, or prospect.

"Nearly home," Dad always said once we could see the little bridge with the crumpled guardrails a dozen miles west of the border between Zambia and Zimbabwe. The bridge was usually choked with goats. Also, it had taken several structural hits, eighteen-wheelers trying to make the border before dark. Crossing that little bridge was a reminder of the impermanence of everything.

But "nearly home" meant if the little bridge collapsed, or if the car broke down, or if we hit a goat and had to begin negotiating compensation with the goat's many sudden owners, or if the road was washed away in a flash flood, we'd be able to walk from here. "Nearly home" meant you were among your people; you were understood, your passage was assured, and your word was good.

By Dad's standards, "nearly home" meant you were safe.

"Yes, I think it's the final stretch," I said.

I forced open the windows next to Dad's bed; a flurry of houseflies blew in on a current of hot, petrol-scented air. There were blackbirds in an elm tree twenty feet from the window. Their irrepressible chatter and squabbling broke through the droning buzz and hum of the ICU.

"Oh, listen to their happy racket," Mum said, smiling gratefully. She put her hand on Dad's arm then, and leaned forward. "Thank you, Hon," she said. She spoke slowly and clearly, as if trying to get through to him on an old telephone line. "That was quite a ride." Then she looked up at me, blinking rapidly, her SOS eyes. "Do you think he heard me?" she asked.

"Yes, I'm sure he did," I said. "Of course he did."

There was a long pause; the blackbirds chattered and squabbled uninterrupted; it made the room less lonely and Dad's impending death more commonplace, as if he were merely resting in a garden somewhere, waiting for a meeting. Death would gently settle next to him then, slide into his place, surely; Death wouldn't alter the mise-en-scène unduly.

The birds would keep up their chorus.

Then night would fall.

Mum sighed. She put her hand on Dad's forehead. A slim rim of tears brimmed in her eyes, but did not fall. "Good-bye, Hon," she said very softly. She stared and stared at him, and then blinked at me again. "I suppose we should go now," she said. "We can't stay here forever."

Then quite suddenly but slowly, very slowly, Dad's hand moved, as if the weight of his still powerfully muscled arm were extraordinary. Slowly, slowly, he reached up for Mum's face; the way he must have done hundreds of times in their fifty-one years together. Mum sat utterly still, her eyes closed.

He touched her hair first. Then he worked his way down her forehead, her arched brows, those cheekbones, that chiseled nose; as if her legendary beauty were one of his beloved old maps he'd pored over, tracing every river and contour, before heading out into the bush and getting completely lost anyway.

From her jawline, he ran his forefinger across her chin until he met the little cleft in the middle, then he gave a tap. "Chin up, Tub," he may as well have said the words, his final instruction to her. And at last her lips, he slowly ran his fingers over her lips, back and forth until she smiled; her final gift to him.

I GOT THE CALL in my hotel room at dawn, Dad's favorite time of day; it was the very sunburned young doctor, I recognized his voice. "The father is dead," the very sunburned young doctor informed me. *The* father. The definite article seemed correct. I was already out of bed, and running toward Mum.

The young doctor had sunburned himself waterskiing at a lake near the city. I'd gleaned that piece of information, as I'd surreptitiously learned everything, from the enemy, Jazmin; he was burned behind the knees, shoulders, everywhere. But I'd never been able to figure out his name. Mum, ever the helpful storyteller, had dubbed him Little Péter, to distinguish him from the old doctor, Old Péter. We liked Old Péter. "So dedicated," Mum said. "So sympathetic."

But I'd disliked Little Péter on sight for all sorts of reasons: For a start, I didn't trust a doctor who'd fry himself like an egg this late in the summer. Also, he'd seemed to be in cahoots with Jazmin; how else would she know exactly how he'd sunburned himself, and where? But Mum was inclined to show a kindly disposition toward Little Péter. I thought it was simply that she hadn't been around him enough to establish a proper prejudice.

I put her in a taxi, her hand tiny around a cup of sweet tea.

She never took sugar, except for shock. She looked so alone, so terrified.

"I'll see you there," I said.

Her eyelids fluttered at me, dash-dot-dash-dot. I wished I'd had a comforting pet I could throw onto her lap.

"Don't worry," I said. "I'll have it all sorted by the time you get there."

Then I ran the four miles from the hotel to the hospital. There were so many refugees now, thousands of people walking through the streets, the city was in gridlock even so early, no one talking. It didn't sound like people on the move. It sounded like the clattering of pigeon wings, or like fat raindrops on a tin roof.

What grief.

I couldn't even begin to fathom what grief. Grief upon grief, I imagined; I couldn't comprehend how a body can withstand losing so much at once, and more with each step, nationless, homeless, unpeopled by force. But in my own untethered newness to this fresh loss, all I could hear was Dad's insistence; he'd made sure the words would stay in my head.

He'd been a lucky man.

No, not just lucky, a very lucky man.

He'd been very lucky, and I was very lucky too.

CHAPTER TWO

When in Doubt, Have a Cigarette

Even this early, people were already smoking in the streets. Budapest, city of smokers; people working a long preoccupation out of their lungs, that's how it seemed. Not the refugees; they were moving, heads down, a people in a terrible hurry to get nowhere. I was moving with my head down too; I wasn't smoking either.

I had quit several days earlier; we were all supposed to have quit. "You should all stop smoking," Dad had suddenly declared in the middle of dying. He had said this quite clearly, although it had taken some effort for him to come to the surface of his comingled worlds to the one in his section of the ICU ward in Budapest; there were visitors unseen to me with whom he was also holding conversations.

Everyone talking at once, Dad hated that; he'd blown out his hearing in the war. He preferred one person talking at a time, or ideally, silence. "Bobo?"

"Dad?"

Dad had motioned me closer; the BBC productions of royal

family shenanigans have this part right, everyone straining to hear the last directives of the dying monarch. Dad paused magnificently. He had my full attention. He'd always had my full attention, from the beginning of my awareness he'd had my full attention.

"You must all stop smoking," Dad had said. Then he'd sunk back against the pillows with a sigh. "Make sure you tell them, Bobo." The directive clearly had exhausted him, because Dad closed his eyes for a while and appeared to be resting; then the other worlds washed back in, and Dad resumed mumbled conversations with visitors invisible to me.

You must all stop smoking.

It wasn't a huge ask, all things considered. We didn't have to restore our father's lost fortunes, defend his character, or redeem his reputation: That might have taken some doing. We simply had to stop smoking.

We'd all smoked like whores on fire, Dad, Van, and I. Rich could outsmoke us all when he showed up; that was worth noting. Mum had tried smoking a few times, valiantly; she stained her fingers a greasy yellow and nearly died of asthma each time. "Oh no. I was *forced* to quit smoking years ago, thank you," she'll tell anyone who offers her a cigarette. "It nearly killed me, but you go right ahead."

We smoked in the car, we smoked in the sitting room, we smoked in the kitchen, we smoked in the bathtub. There were ashtrays everywhere; that was Mum's contribution, she collected them, she bought them, she stole them. "I refuse to be one of those boring ex-smokers who becomes holier than thou when they stop," Mum said, holiest of them all.

My father smoked one cigarette after the other; a pungent grey ribbon of burning tobacco followed him wherever he went;

he could light a cigarette while driving a motorbike in deep sand, you don't see that very often. I smoked like my father, although after I married Charlie—"An American," Mum said with grim satisfaction, "she'll be forced to quit"—I quit.

"It's frowned upon in America," Mum expounded; much of what she knows about the United States she's picked up from the BBC World Service and from the advertisements in American airline magazines when she's come to visit the children and me in Wyoming. "They're very keen on their health over there. And they're fanatical about white teeth."

I still smoked in my dreams, though. And I smoked when I came home to Zambia. Also I smoked on assignment for magazines and newspapers, when I was out of the country. Angola, Zimbabwe, Haiti, Mozambique, South Africa; wherever there's suffering, there're cigarettes. I bought the roughest, the cheapest. I bought cartons; I bought to share. We were always up against it, deadlines, dust, and failing light. We smoked when we were tired, hungry, or anxious.

"Lung snack anyone?"

The health warnings on the back of the cigarette packs and tobacco tins didn't deter us then; we read them at roadblocks, in hotel rooms, and in our camps—hours kicking around waiting for an interview, or waiting for something to happen, or hoping nothing would. Dad didn't heed the health warnings either. "Well, Bobo, if smoking's what finally kills me it'll be a bloody miracle," he said.

There were so many alternatives; it would be a miracle.

Nicotine Tim they'd called Dad at the expensive, mediocre English boarding school he'd attended in the fifties. But smoking for my father was never just about the addiction, although there was that too. "Filthy habit," he'd say occasionally, but he'd never quit for long, only temporarily, when forced by regulations, say, or a very high fever.

In my father's world, tobacco was a way to get around. It was bribes to policemen and customs officials. It was solace to soldiers. It was instead of a meal when food had run out. It was a way to meet a stranger. It was how to defuse mistrust. Cigarettes were what you did when there was nothing else to be done.

But there was something unnatural about it too. "Never forget that tobacco is a fourteen-month crop," Dad told me once. "There's no time to rest." It was an aberrant harvest; hard on soil, untethered from time. And for him, everything was about time, burning through it the way he did.

Smoked properly, a cigarette to my father was a way to slow time down. At a dinner party, a cigarette between courses was companionable; a way to permit the food to settle, an interval to allow conversations that may have overheated to cool and those that may have cooled to warm up.

"Anyone care to join me for intercourse?" Dad would ask, pushing himself back from the table after the soup but before the meat. Or after the meat but before the pudding he'd shout, "*Garçon!*" As if all waiters—even waiters in Zambia—were French, regardless of the more likely scenario, which was that they weren't. "Rectify this drought! We're all going outside for a breath of fresh air!"

Then we drifted outside, following Dad, our glasses refreshed, fresh cigarettes lit; and the air in the car parks, or gardens, or streets felt suddenly invigorating, our perspectives renewed, everything a little more romantic; insects calling, frogs, always something scuttling off into the undergrowth in that part of the world, small mammals up trees, or a gecko laughing from the walls beneath electric lights.

"Let's have a party!" That was Dad's war cry.

Mum would stiffen slightly. "Someone's restless tonight," she'd observe, but the corners of her mouth would be twitching with happy anticipation.

"Olé!" Dad would shout from across the lawn.

"Olé!" Mum would cry, head thrown back.

Then after a while, someone sensible would notice the mosquitoes were out in force, and that we were all being chewed to death. We'd all clatter inside, another round of drinks! "Join us! Have a drink!" my father would shout to patrons at other tables. "Bring your women!" That was a dinner party with my father, a wonderful host, and a siren call to a crashing hangover.

Or the way my father called it, a proper religious experience.

THERE'S ONE IN EVERY PROPER FAMILY—or there should be—a black sheep. There are also aunts in every proper family, or there used to be. Dad had five; one behind every rock in England, he complained. "Tim Fuller went to Africa and lost everything," the aunts had lamented. It wasn't what they'd hoped; it wasn't what he'd given them to expect. He'd had his larks.

He'd done the usual spell in Paris before college; he'd sown a wild oat or two on the Continent, where no one spoke proper English and everyone was foreign, so it didn't matter. He'd earned his diploma, barely. He'd kidnapped the Dairy Queen on graduation day.

It was time for him to settle down.

"But I knew I couldn't stay in England," Dad said. "It was already too small and crowded without me cluttering up the place." Instead, he took off for Canada and hired on as a farmhand in Quebec. "In those days the Canadians paid the passage over plus fifty quid for anyone who'd go out and whiten the place up a bit," Dad said. "Biting flies in summer, deadly winters."

When he'd had enough of the cold—"Didn't take very long," Dad said, "terrible bloody climate"—he found work at a hotel in the West Indies. Rum punches, sun, and goat stew; he was happy there, but when his bar bill exceeded his salary he took it as a sign he'd outstayed his welcome and applied for a job on a wattle plantation in Kenya, where he also planned to see a giraffe. He always said that: "I wanted to go to Kenya to see a giraffe."

But before he could see a giraffe, Dad set eyes on Mum. She'd recently returned to Kenya after a mandatory year in London. She'd hated every moment of it. She'd loathed the weather, and she'd found the people intolerant of her colonial accent. "One flat vowel and they pounced," Mum said. "Ridiculous, of course. I have perfect RP." She paused. "Received Pronunciation. The way the BBC used to be before they went all funny."

Mum had come back to her parents' farm on the Uasin Gishu plateau, back to her beloved mare Violet, back to her unfettered life under perfect equatorial light. She was determined to make up for lost time. "Well, she's your mother," Dad said. "I don't need to tell you what happens when she gets the bit between her teeth."

Mum had been raised with the highlands, horses, and homemade wine beneath the gaze of Mount Elgon in neighboring Uganda. "We led very wholesome, outdoorsy lives in Keen-ya," Mum said, glancing down at her very good legs; her calves have always slid without protest into the slimmest of slim riding boots. "It was obvious to Dad right away. We were having much more fun in East Africa than anyone was having in the dreary old Home Counties."

Now that he was self-exiled to the ex-colonies, my father's family hardly spoke to him or of him again, although it's not as if he was able to shake off his past. The pettiness of the dreary old Home Counties trailed him to Kenya too, of course it did. There was always, is still, a question of one's pedigree; a concept so British it ingrained itself and lodged and festered wherever the British were, wherever they went. "The aunts were hoping to select a wife from the pages of the *Who's Who*," Dad said. "Although by the time I got to the West Indies, they'd have settled for anything with a double-barreled name as long as it was white."

Similarly, when after less than a month in Kenya, Dad rashly proposed to Mum, there were frantic letters from my maternal grandmother in Eldoret to relatives back in Britain. "Name of Timothy Fuller, mother née Garrard, the Crown Jewelers. Father's side is navy," Granny wrote to her sister, Flora, still living near the ancestral home on the Isle of Skye. "He seems all right. But as he's not from any family we know, many questions remain dangling."

And for the most part, they remained dangling. My father's side of the family didn't attend his wedding nor did they ever visit him afterward in our large, loose, scrappy lives. It was as if Dad had pitched up in Kenya attached to nothing, an English foundling under his own recognizance, lost abroad. Tim Fuller of No Fixed Abode, he declared himself.

ON JULY 10, 1964, seven months after they met, my parents were married in Eldoret, Kenya. Mum a day over twenty, Dad barely twenty-four. The men wore top hats and tails, the women wore gloves, girls from the local high school sang in the choir; unremarkably conventional nuptials except for what happened next.

"I think your father mistook the sound of a champagne cork for the sound of a starting gun," my grandmother said afterward.

"Your parents took off for their honeymoon at a hundred miles an hour, and they never slowed down for the corners."

By the time I was born, five years into their marriage, Mum and Dad had already lived on several farms in three countries on two continents; they'd even been jauntily homeless for a bit in Rhodesia when Vanessa was a baby and Mum pregnant, living out of a car. That baby, a son, had died of meningitis; he'd been nine months old.

My parents were on the next train to Beira.

A brief stint in England, then back to Rhodesia, then to Malawi, and finally Zambia, my parents moved and moved. Vanessa and I tried to add it all up once, twenty times or more we moved, for all sorts of reasons—political upheaval, market vagaries, drought, a funny feeling my mother had, a weekend's bad fishing, my father's restlessness, disease in the crops, and after the deaths, one by one, of three of their five children.

Each dislodgment must have panicked Mum; but somehow she'd model every crumbling farmhouse or converted barn into something homey and familiar. Over and over again with nearly undiminished energy, she rerooted our peripatetic little family, always the four of us, a pack of dogs, sometimes a couple of cats.

"Very clever curtains she made wherever she went," an old family friend reminded me recently. I remembered that—the curtains made of tobacco sacking, bordered with cheap cheerful cotton; the tablecloths made of calico sheets. Mum stitched our way into new homes over and over; she kept us sewn together, she threaded us into place.

She'd done it here too; her Budapest hotel room was beginning to resemble one of our homes. There was her little library, her books from home smothered in Blue Death. Blue Death is an insecticide made for markets that have not yet got around to banning it, guaranteed to turn insects into exoskeletons on the spot. Mum loves it; she drops it into conversation here and there, as if Blue Death were her official sponsor.

Next to her library, there was her tea station, her drinks tray, an ugly white ashtray advertising a boat cruise on the Danube. "Dad made a fuss when I was trying to stuff that into my handbag," Mum had said. "But now at least I have a memento of our last excursion together before he collapsed, poor Dad."

"That's very romantic," I'd said.

"Yes," Mum had said. "Very. I don't know if Dad had fun, though. You know how he is. He always looks sour when I make him do touristy things; he doesn't like to be told what to look at, and he doesn't like being told interesting facts. In Hungary, for example, they call it the Duna River. That's almost more poetic, isn't it? Duna. Our last excursion was on the Duna River. I like that; it sounds mysterious. They gave a very informative presentation." She'd paused. "Dad pretended to sleep throughout."

I NEVER DID SEE THE DUNA, the Blue Danube, although the hospital was only a few blocks away. But I could feel it, the city pulled toward it, the way most cities are drawn to and built from their water. "If you're ever lost, walk downhill," Dad had always said. "Eventually you'll find a river."

"What if it's flat where I'm lost?"

"Then keep going until you find a hill," Dad had said.

As I got closer to the hospital, and to the river, toward the ancient inner city, its narrow cobbled streets made for a different world, the press of refugees thinned. Now, instead of a mass of humanity, there were scattered clusters of people, like tragic little birds broken off from the main migratory group, but it didn't lessen the weight of their sorrow.

Grief is like weather when it's held by so many; a grief cell, a grief cloud, a grief front. An area of grief stalled now, for the moment, over Budapest; stalled, not ended. And there was no end in sight.

Grief is not a landing place.

Unlike the past and death, grief isn't another country; it's a place between countries, a holding pattern, a purgatory. I didn't know what expression to assume. "I'm so sorry for your loss," I wanted to say over and over, as if I were at a hundred funerals. "I'm sorry for your many, many losses."

Unlike me, Dad would have known the correct demeanor in these circumstances; the reasonable balance between the little grief of one timely death and the tidal grief of these exiles. "Put everything in perspective, Bobo," Dad always said.

In perspective, Dad would have seen the whole. He'd have seen his one well-used life draining away versus the blood of whole countries draining away, lives and livelihoods; identities tattered like ribbons. People are people until they're a people. Then they move as a single entity, insolubly bonded by their shared trauma.

"Where's the Red Cross?" I'd thought. "The aid workers."

Dad would never have looked for the do-gooders; he hated do-gooders. He'd have done the correct thing instinctively. He'd have done what he could to mitigate a reality that was older than all centuries and bigger than all lands. "Have a cigarette," he'd have said. "Let me light that for you."

And everyone would have been disburdened for a moment while cigarettes were lit, smoke exhaled into the unkind air, sighs exchanged. "It looks like you might be in for a long day," Dad may have commented, looking at the morning sun, new in the sky but already pale and hot. "Here, you'd better take the whole pack."

Cigarettes are not the way to extend life; that wasn't my father's goal or concern. He wasn't doling out longevity; he was doling out endurance. Endurance was one of his signature characteristics. He could keep going strong long after lesser men and women had slid unceremoniously under the table.

"Man down!" Dad would shout. "Someone, administer the kiss of life. What? Must I do everything myself?" Now he was man down too, slid under the table, and there was no one to bring him back. He was gone, and a time had gone with him, and my way of knowing how to be in all time; that too had vanished.

So this is grief, I'd thought.

It's the theft of time, all time for all of time.

CHAPTER THREE

Befriend the Moon

There is a difference, I found, between a hospital housing your sick, and one in which you imagine vividly your dead is lying, tagged like you see in movies, on a slab in the basement mortuary. *Timothy Donald Fuller. Born unremarkably March 9, 1940, Northampton, England. Died improbably September 4, 2015, Pest, Hungary.*

Until yesterday, I'd viewed this rambling, ugly hospital as a temporary holding station in which my father was serving out an inevitable sentence in a hot, strange, sad city with me as witness. But the fact of his dying had changed the shape of everything. Now the building was a monument to his death. Dad's final breaths taken here, his soul untangling from flesh within these walls.

His determinedly good death, his noble suffering had visited grandeur where previously there'd been only a kind of surrendered sadness, a rotation of bodies, washing in and out of view. I'd had too much of a colonial upbringing, and my father had been too English, for Rupert Brooke not to tumble unbidden into my head.

"If I should die, think only this of me: / That there's some corner of a foreign field / That is for ever England."

But neither my father nor I was so deluded to think an Englishman's blood was enough to stain the soil of any nation richer, or that dying somewhere as a soldier, or a civilian, or a refugee, or a tourist made that land yours no matter how much you'd suffered on it, or for it. Nothing seemed that certain anymore, such claims were fighting words, words to get lost by; and certainly not the reassurance I was seeking.

Still, a few days ago, back when he'd still been laboring toward death, and shouting instructions in his morphine haze to Mr. Kalusha, the farm's driver, to hurry home before dark, I'd given semiserious thought to getting my father in the back of a rental van and making a break for it with him, driving east from Hungary, then south to Gibraltar. I'd have opened the van doors; propped my father up as close as I could to the strait. On a clear day he might have seen Africa one last time.

I'd have fed him brandy; he'd have died in Mum's arms.

Or he'd have died in no one's arms; that's someone else's family. But at least Mum and I could have been fussing with the picnic basket; cursing the lid to the thermos; fighting off a troop of Barbary macaques in the vicinity. He might have died then, gazing south from Europe toward his beloved farm, a familiar, cheerful chaos in the background, Mum shrieking at some monkeys.

That would have been a fathomable death for me, a more coherent inscription in my mind: *Timothy Donald Fuller, born unremarkably March 9, 1940, England. Died within sight of Africa, September 4, 2015.* But it doesn't work like that, of course: Death comes where it comes, and when it comes, and it doesn't wait around for any man, wife, parent, or daughter to announce his or her readiness for it.

There's no planning for the perfect death, or rather, there is, but there's no planning for the perfect aftershock of a loved one's death. The assault of it is always new, always, each grief finding a new wormhole into our hearts. Like all life's shocks, beginning with our own unasked-for births, there's no guarding against the shock of sorrow, the shock of losing parts of the self.

And death, like birth, afterward everything's a first. A long pileup of firsts. The first decisions I'd be making on Dad's departed behalf; the first true uncertainty about whom I'd become with his death, because until now, whatever else I'd been, I'd always also been Tim Fuller's daughter, and that had really meant something in one or two places.

The Chirundu market, for example, where Dad did all his farm shopping, he'd be sorely missed there. Also the little safari lodge on the Kafue River, they'd notice he was gone. Of course Boss Shupi would look for him in vain every morning at eleven for the remainder of the dry season.

And they'd never forget my father at Huey's Pub and Grill in Lusaka, where in recent memory Dad had set his trousers on fire, dancing on the table over wilting paraffin candles. "I was led astray by a Malawian waiter," my father explained in his defense. "Three Irish whiskies after a fulsome dinner. Of course I got a bit overexcited."

I STOOD ALONE at the locked doors of the ICU, peering through the small, greasy panes of glass into the dim hall beyond. I rang the bell and waited. After a few minutes, I rang the bell again. Bodies in green scrubs floated around in the frame of the scummy glass, emerging into the fluorescent glare of the hallway only to submerge out of it again into dark rooms.

I rang the bell, longer this time, really leaning on it. I heard myself saying lines from American movies, "Who is supposed to be in charge here?" "Does anyone know what's going on?" But those not raised in North America know these are absurd things to say in countries that are still getting accustomed to the free market's stated assertion that the customer is always right.

No Zambian would make this mistake.

Mum, for example, who although an avowed anti-communist has spent most of her life under various socialist regimes in southern Africa. She thought the Hungarian hospital was a model operation; the sort of place where the customer is always not only automatically assumed to be wrong but also willfully stupid. "This place is top-notch," she'd insisted, wheezing as she'd hauled herself up the stairs in the terrible heat. "State of the art."

I rang the bell again, hammered on the doors.

Behind me, a row of patients in worn pajamas sagged on wooden benches, more vulnerable-looking than if they had been completely naked; the faded little flowers on mildly stained gowns, the manly plaid stripes imagined for livelier legs, the frills meant for younger necks. They all looked much more corpselike than Dad had just twelve hours earlier, and yet here they were, and here he wasn't.

And at least in their country of sickness, the Hungarian patients made a little village, a community; they were richer than I was in that regard. Their united babble of a language like no tongue I'd ever heard before translated in my mind as a kind of absurd theatricality. As if, dying, they'd come to practice this noise on one another in preparation for the language they'd use in the next world.

"It's one of the Uralic family of languages, so called because of the mountains," Mum had informed me when I'd complained to her about the alphabet, forty-four strange, extended letters; words hatched with diacritical marks. It was impossible for me to make anything of any street signs or notices. She'd done her research, of course, long conversations at the front desk. "I find it rather romantic," she'd said.

"Which mountains?" I'd asked.

"The Urals, obviously. Goodness, Bobo, who was your poor geography teacher? It's very specific to the region; the Hungarian language, I mean, like Finnish. The rules are extremely complicated and there are lots of exceptions. The accusative suffix is a nasal sound, apparently."

"The accusative suffix?" I'd repeated.

Mum had regarded me with diminishing hope, her shoulders dropping. "Did you retain none of the elements of grammar?"

"Mrs. Fryer hated me," I'd reminded her.

"Yes, well," Mum had said.

I BATTERED THE DOORS, rang the bell.

It was as if I'd ceased to exist, as if my father's death had taken me with him. "It'll be all right in the end," Dad used to say. "If it isn't all right, it isn't the end." But this wasn't the end I had in mind; that made it harder to accept, as did the fact that dozens of spells of malaria, a war, and the road to Lusaka hadn't killed my father, but a sudden bout of pneumonia had snatched him off, same as any other common old mortal person.

Six months earlier on the farm, one night before supper, when Dad had hit the sweet spot of his second brandy, lots of water, no ice, he'd said, "Let me tell you the secret to life right now, in case

I suddenly give up the ghost." Then he lit his pipe and stroked Harry's head. Harry put his paw on Dad's lap and they sat there, the two of them, one man and his dog, keepers to the secret of life.

"Well?" I said.

"Nothing comes to mind, quite honestly, Bobo," Dad said, looking at me with some surprise. "Now that I think about it, maybe there isn't a secret to life. It's just what it is, right under your nose. What do you think, Harry?" Harry gave Dad a look of utter agreement. He was a very superior dog. "Well, there you have it," Dad said.

I laughed. Mrs. Hilda Tembo, in the kitchen overseeing the roasting of one of Mum's lambs, also laughed. Mum was in the bath listening to opera. From the radio on top of the low wall that more or less divided the kitchen from not-the-kitchen, the BBC chattered on, companionably static; choruses of frogs kicked up a racket in the wetlands at the bottom of the garden.

I remember thinking then, my father couldn't give up the ghost. Or he'd die eventually, of course, everyone does, but surely he'd die like a tree. He'd remain standing, casting cool shade on all of us on hot days, offering us fuel for warmth with his breaking branches on cold nights; he'd petrify like those fossilized forests near the Muchinga Escarpment. He'd be forever preserved a rose-colored pink, but he couldn't be gone.

Except now he was.

"COR BLIMEY, IT'S 'OT."

I swung around, the terrible attempt at a Cockney accent was unmistakable; Mum suddenly appeared on the landing. She stopped to take a few puffs from her inhaler. "Those stairs," she gasped. "Very good exercise." She looked oxygen deprived, also she'd shrunk about six inches since I'd put her in the taxi in the hotel what felt like hours ago, two at least. It was midmorning now. "Luckily I keep myself very fit. Walking the dogs, you know."

She staggered up to me, steadied herself on my arm, wiped her brow and cleared her throat; a boxer between rounds. "It's about ninety degrees out there already, Fahrenheit," she reported. "And all the streets are completely jammed. Did you see? The taxi simply had to crawl along to get here." Then she frowned at the locked doors, glanced at her watch. "Have you been here this whole time? And you couldn't get in? Where's Little Péter?"

"Yes," I said. "I have. And no. I don't know. I've hammered on the doors. I've rung the bell. I've hammered on the doors some more. I was beginning to wonder if I'd died myself."

Mum rolled her eyes. "Oh, don't be silly, Bobo." She gave the door a testing nudge, then she lowered her voice: "The thing you need to remember about these old locks"—she paused and glanced furtively over her shoulder at the sagging patients on the bench behind us—"is that they're susceptible to a good shove."

And then that diminished, bereft woman, my mum, barely a bird of her former self, hauled back and quietly, but firmly, crashed the doors to the ICU open. "Phew," she said. She took a couple more draws off her inhaler, then serenely closed the doors behind us.

"That, Bobo," she said, "is communist-era construction for you. You'd never see that in America." She looked at me then, pityingly, as if my life had been dimmed by mere dint of the fact that half of it had taken place in the United States, a country that had defined itself in large part by its opposition to all things communist, thereby denying its citizens and immigrants the chance to experience communism's exciting difficulties firsthand. "That is why Budapest is my kind of place," Mum said. "We understand each other." She squared her shoulders. "Right," she said. "Best foot forward."

With sudden shock, I realized Mum had already committed this dreadful humid hospital to her memory as one of the finest institutions; she'd already made courageous peace with this moment; she'd already decided to make friends with this city where her husband had died.

"Budapest! It has a ring to it, doesn't it?" Mum said. "Who hasn't invaded this place? The Mongols, the Turks, the Nazis, the Russians, and last but not least, Tim Fuller the Hon. *Requiescat in pace!*"

I felt suspended in a Stefan Zweig novel.

It was the Middle Eastern refugees, the Hungarian patients waiting for death, the freshly widowed ex-colonial crashing her way into the hospital ward where earlier in the story her husband had died far from his people; his people twice removed—there was always the question of my father's people. I was never sure who they were, exactly.

That seemed very Stefan Zweig too.

"If nothing else," Mum was continuing, "Budapest's not a boring place to die."

Then suddenly, down the corridor, Little Péter walked out of an office and into the gloomy hall; his gauzy green scrubs puffed out in great billows, the surgical-garb equivalent of Princess Di's wedding dress. "Ah!" Mum gave a shout of happy surprise. "There you are, Little Péter!" Little Péter froze in his tracks. In the burned-out fluorescent light, he looked like a swollen green bovine in the mist; bewildered.

"Ah," he said.

"And here I am!" Mum said as she hurried toward him. She planted herself in front of Little Péter and seized him by both shoulders. "Remember me? I'm Mrs. Fuller. My husband was your patient, Mr. Fuller." She paused importantly; she was splendid. "I am the widow." She gave his shoulders a reassuring squeeze.

Little Péter winced; I'd calculated second-degree burns at least, and now those sheets of bubbling, blistered skin covering his shoulders were in Mum's viselike grip. "Yes, I know," Mum said. "I know, but we did ring the bell. And, well, we did knock," Mum explained. "Didn't we, Bobo? Then we rang the bell some more, but there wasn't an answer. So then we gave the door a tiny nudge."

Little Péter repressed a yelp.

"No, no, no," Mum said. "We're not all upset, are we, Bobo? It's a miracle he survived so long."

There was a low moan.

"Oh, dear," Mum said. She was rubbing Little Péter's arms vigorously now, the way you'd rub down a sweating horse. Another yelp ensued. "You really mustn't blame yourself, Little Péter. My husband had a very full life, very."

I thought I saw a tear roll down Little Péter's nose, although since he was also sweating profusely, and the light was poor, it was hard to tell. It was a pretty dreadful spectacle anyway. I can see where Mum lost her nerve, honestly.

"Um," Mum said, her voice quavering with uncertainty. She turned to me. "He's falling apart a bit," she said, sotto voce.

"I'm not sure he understands English very well," I said.

"Oh, right," Mum said. "Of course! How stupid of me." She turned back to Little Péter, her face set in her best Memsahib Abroad expression. "We will leave you to get on with your rounds now," she said slowly and loudly. "A great man . . ." Mum paused. "A good man," she amended with hard-won modesty, "has died, and we will all just have to get on with our lives without him now."

Little Péter gargled.

"Yes, all of us," Mum said, fixing Little Péter with a look supposed to restore all our dignities. "Thank you so very much." And then, in determined Hungarian, continuing to massage Little Péter's arm through his scrubs as she did so, *"Köszönöm."*

Little Péter looked close to complete breakdown.

"Oh, dear"—Mum looked at me—*"köszönöm szépen.* It's supposed to mean 'Thank you very much.' I asked the concierge."

Little Péter slipped Mum's grip.

"Oh, I'm so sorry," Mum said. "Of course, you must be very busy. Well, don't let us keep you. My daughter will be in touch about the . . . My daughter will be in touch concerning the details. Won't you, Bobo?"

I nodded.

"Good. Well, that's that, then." Mum's far stronger than she looks. She gave Little Péter one last, terrifying smile, then marched us both out of the swing doors, back into the corridor. "Little Péter looked shocked to the absolute quick, poor man," she said, hurrying me as fast as her asthma would allow down the stairs. "Positively feverish with emotion."

"He's severely sunburned," I said.

Mum stopped for a moment, and regarded me with mild surprise. "Is he?"

"You could see it for yourself," I said.

"No, I couldn't," Mum said. "He was covered head to toe in surgical togs."

"He did it waterskiing on his day off," I said.

"Well, why didn't you say something?" Mum asked.

"It didn't seem newsworthy," I said. "At the time."

Mum hobbled down a few more steps. "Well," she said. "I still think Little Péter was very moved by Dad's death. Very. We all are;

everyone is. I'm sure he shed a tear or two; I could swear I thought I saw tears."

"Me too," I said.

And then we were outside again. Mum stalled to catch her breath and to bid each cat farewell by name. "Marmalade," on account of her stripes; "Greedy," for obvious reasons; "Sponge Bob," on account of his yellowish square pants. They emerged at the sound of her voice, more and more cats. "What a handsome fellow," Mum crooned, crouching down, the better to ensure no one was being left out of the conversation. "Oh, hello, Kanga."

After that, there was a whole exchange with the gateman; Mum leafing over a little pile of cash so he'd feed the cats when she was gone. "Sometimes you just have to believe in the kindness of strangers," she told me, methodically counting the notes into the gateman's outstretched hand; Mum always manages to look furtive around money, like someone involved in a drug deal. "You really do, Bobo."

There were pools of surprised and grateful tears in the gateman's eyes; I could already tell the cats weren't going to be fed. But this was where Mum's deep suspicion of humans failed her. Or rather, her deep suspicion remained firmly lodged, but her nearly incredible affinity for animals overrode all her normal prejudices and reservations.

"He'll probably drink it," she said. "But that's all right. We all need a little anesthetic from time to time."

Mum could charm birds from trees, chameleons ceased their hissing in her presence, and snakes sunbathed placidly in her garden. Animals adored her, she loved animals, and she pre-forgave anyone whom she perceived as being a fellow animal lover, regardless of things that would ordinarily have them struck from her consideration: a fault in their religion, ethnicity, or class, for example.

Mum and the gateman were smiling and patting each other. *"Isten áldja meg,"* Mum said. Then turning to me, "It means 'God bless you.' I learned that from the concierge too. They're very Catholic around here, you know." The gateman patted the top of Mum's head, the way a person might pat a dog; it was a memorable gesture. Mum smiled and patted the gateman on the cheek in return, the way she might comfort a horse.

Then we left.

OUT IN THE STREETS the day continued, hot and oppressive. It seemed to me the world should have stopped altogether; its gaskets blown, its gears stripped, its engine on blocks. Instead it felt merely stalled, as if something urgent still might happen, a thunderstorm, for example, or a riot. The world hadn't ended when Dad did and it wasn't pausing for him; it was pausing for itself.

Mum was wheezing worse than ever, walking haltingly. "You know, Bobo," she said as we trudged the city block that encompassed the crumbling hospital, "I really do think it's worth remembering . . . Oh, look at all the starlings, over there, on the steeple, like dark emeralds in the sun. Do you see them?"

I looked for the gemlike birds.

"Very shiny," I agreed. "Oh look, there's more over there."

But Mum was continuing. "I think it's worth remembering, it was really a very good death, Bobo. It wasn't bad. Not bad at all." The starlings took wing, churning in the hazy sky as a single entity; they whirred and planed on hot currents; ash from a wildfire behaves in a similar way.

"But he died alone," I blurted out, wishing I could unsay the words even as they were falling from my lips. "Alone, in a strange city, away from everything he loved."

"Mm," Mum said; she stopped and clung on to a nearby rusty railing that was demarking the sidewalk from a chalk-dry fountain, a melting parking lot, and the hospital laboratories. She took a puff from her inhaler. "Yes, Bobo. Put that way, it does sound horrible and desperate."

Mum cleared her throat. She refuses to wallow in the past, however recent. "Did you see the moon last night?" she asked, giving her chest a bit of a thump. She straightened her shoulders and continued up the sidewalk. I straightened my shoulders and followed her.

Mum excels at this: She excels at the next thing.

Her supremely agile mind is ready to change the topic away from the unpleasant toward the soothing at any moment. To this end, it's been stuffed to the brim with the essentials; old maps, home remedies, a remnant of Swahili, the latest news from the BBC, serviceable Nyanja, advanced first aid, self-taught snake and bird identification. An emergency store of detailed weather reports, witty pet anecdotes, and recent planetary observations is updated and refreshed regularly. She's made a link somewhere, a butterfly mind, a magpie mind, a fox mind; nectar, shiny objects, cats.

"Yes," I said. "I saw the moon last night."

Mum smiled. "A blood moon," she said.

I nodded. "I know."

Unable to sleep, I'd sat at the window of my hotel room and watched the moon go down over the city, a ponderous red globe. It was only natural my mother had seen the moon too; she'd have opened the curtains to the little balcony where she'd strung up her laundry and sat there to watch it, taking in the hot city's thick night air.

Both my parents could always tell you the phase of the moon without needing to see it; without glancing skyward, they just knew. Of course they did; farmers, fishermen, soldiers acutely observe the sky.

Waxing, crescent, waning, gibbous, blue, full, new.

"A blood moon was Dad's favorite, you know," Mum said. "I think that's very auspicious. Although a new moon is supposed to be very lucky too, unless you see it through glass, and then it's very unlucky. Did you know that? Yes, of course you knew that. You're supposed to turn money over in your pocket and bow seven times when you see a new moon. It's supposed to make you rich."

"Yes, I knew that," I said.

I knew Mum turned money over in her pocket and bowed seven times whenever there was a new moon; running out into the garden, or hopping out of the car to avoid seeing it through glass. I could never see a new moon without thinking of the fortune it owed Mum.

And I would never see another blood moon without thinking of Dad. I worked it out from the medical records afterward; he'd died soon after moonset. I wondered then if he'd lain awake in those final hours and seen the moonrise late—red and slow and sorrowful—the way Mum and I had. I wondered if he had seen it sliding past the outline of this unfamiliar cityscape, setting behind domes and turrets. And if then, as Mum must have suspected, he'd slipped away with her, his old friend, a blood moon, a harvester's moon, not alone at all.

CHAPTER FOUR

Sometimes, You Just Have to Bite the Bullet

D ad had shot pheasant in England; he had done a little deer stalking in Scotland; he'd nearly frozen to death in a duck blind in Quebec. "I was forced to be sober for the entire twelve-hour ordeal," Dad remembered with a shudder decades later. "It turned out, they were *dry* Canadians. I think that's the closest I've come to a gun-related fatality in my life, and that's up against some stiff competition."

The war had been one thing. But the war bled into everything else, at least for a few years. The earliest of my father's hunting companions that I could remember were left over from the war; I'd never known them not slung about with arms. The Brothers H. had been our neighbors in the valley; they were part of Dad's unit on patrol.

"We always started at the Impala Arms, and two weeks later, we were supposed to end up at Leopard's Rock," Dad said. "Those two pubs were the really dangerous parts of the war, although the bits in between could get quite hairy too."

The Brothers H. never let Dad forget that he was English.

They made him walk forty paces behind and sleep eighty paces downwind; he snored and left unmistakable bandy-legged Englishman spoor. They, on the other hand, were poster-child Rhodesians; their father had been the first white settler to reach the valley, with all that implies.

They could navigate by the stars, and they'd been tracking and hunting big game since toddlerhood. None of the Brothers H. was what could be described as dry; one of them drank like the aunts. "At least I didn't have to choose between drunkenness and death," Dad had said. "With those three, I could have both."

The mother of the Brothers H. was the grandest woman I've ever known; she seems imaginary now when I think of her peculiarities. She spoke the Queen's English; she used an ebony cigarette holder; she piled her silver hair into an Edwardian bun secured with an ivory comb. Her husband, the father of the Brothers H., had died before we moved to the valley—malaria, I think; a fever of some sort, I believe—but not before naming everything he saw after somewhere else.

He'd named the valley Burma. It had been wild jungle then, when he'd first settled it. It was humid too, boiling beneath the misty highlands to the north and west. He'd named the hills bordering Mozambique to the east the Himalayas. The Rhodesian government put in one of the largest minefields in the world along that border.

After the war, the youngest Brother H. was forced at gunpoint to walk across the minefield, although it was technically Zimbabwe's minefield by then; the half-life of war is more indiscriminate than you'd think. He lost the better part of a leg out there that day. "He never once complained," Dad said, impressed with the youngest Brother H. "He didn't even let on he might be a bit disappointed, losing a leg like that."

They weren't high, our Himalayas, but they looked daunting. In memory now, the hills appear to me always smoky purple, as if dryly bruised. But, of course, they weren't always this way. It must have rained. Of course it rained. There were times those hills were verdant, fragrant with wild blooms and iridescent with fresh msasa leaves.

It definitely rained.

Seven cows drowned in a flood once, seven inches it rained that night, an inch for each cow; my cat, Tapioca, died in that storm too. And I know too, there were times of bucolic, lush tranquillity when it had rained just enough, a gentle rain all through the night, and we awoke to find the place washed fresh: red soil, blue sky, and green trees.

We awoke to a sense of peace and possibility and optimism.

We awoke to those things, before fear washed back in.

But I have to deduce my way back to those memories.

IT WASN'T CLEAR WHY MY FATHER went hunting with the Brothers H., or with anyone at all. Dad wasn't interested in trophies. He'd spent a few of his school holidays in the homes of posh, distant relations who'd already plundered the fauna of an empire; tiger rugs in the hall, elephant tusks bracketing the chimneypiece, a surprised leopard snarling on the wall in the smoking room. Dad shot for the pot only, and wasted nothing. He saved every hide; he kept the skulls for Mum's dogs to chew on.

"I'm a harvester, not a hunter," Dad said.

But my father didn't turn down an invitation to hunt, or to do anything almost, on principle. "I'll try anything once," he paraphrased the old adage. "Except buggery, incest, and moderation." It amused the Brothers H. to have Dad along on their expeditions.

They preyed on his English naïveté and his natural propensity for drama. "He lengthened his stride when it would have been more prudent to shorten it," the middle Brother H. told me much later. "It was worth having him along for that reason alone."

The Brothers H. had smirked wordlessly when Dad pitched his tent under a marula tree, the fruit of which is irresistibly intoxicating to elephants; they'd watched from optimal distance, propped up on their rifles, weak with laughter, as a rhino they'd been tracking doubled back and charged Dad, causing him to have to run and dive twenty feet into a dry riverbed.

"Dad's so trusting, he's terribly innocent in a lot of ways. And those rotten brothers were merciless pranksters, always leading poor Dad into serious peril," Mum said. "No wonder he never managed to bag anything larger than a scrawny francolin while he was with them."

But Dad wasn't there for the pursuit of wildlife or to pit himself against their territory. He went because he didn't have a reason not to go; with an open mind, in other words. And he found that he was repaired and restored by the experience; the medicine of such a wild wilderness seemed endless. "The secret to life, I learned it there," he said long afterward, a few brandies into an afternoon session.

"Which was?" I wanted to know.

Dad sat for a long time before shaking his head and looking at me with amused puzzlement. "Sorry, Bobo. I'm a bit assholes, plus I'm getting bloody senile. What was the question again?"

"What's the secret to life?" I reminded him.

"Oh," Dad said, remembering.

––––––––

MY FATHER HAD LEARNED about getting lost and wilderness from the war and from the Brothers H. In turn, I'd learned about war by hapless experience and I had learned about getting lost and wilderness from my father. For example, we'd be six flat tires into an already long day, miles deep in hot camel-thorn country, far from anything remotely resembling a road. "Here is our stop, apparently," Dad would say.

So we'd scramble out of the Land Rover and look around.

"Nice and quiet," Dad would comment; the bush sang with insects and heat. "I bet they have a room for the night."

Then someone would start a small fire; the big black kettle would emerge from the tin trunk. Tents would be set up. The tea, sugar, and powdered milk would be retrieved from the ammo can, maybe we'd find rusks if we were lucky, and if we were very lucky there'd be oranges. Everything we needed within reach.

"Look at me, living like a king," Dad would never fail to notice.

This was the year after the war.

Mum had sunk momentarily beyond reach, understandably.

She'd been far more appalled by the loss of the war than had Dad; unlike him, she hadn't been expecting it. Mum hadn't volunteered for the police reservists, and worn that awful uniform, only to lose in the end. For a start, it hadn't been an easy look to pull off, grey, sanctions-era polyester, not designed to flatter, but Mum had somehow managed to achieve effortless fascist chic; the member in charge, Banquo Brown, had particularly remarked on it.

No one had consulted her about the Lancaster House Agreement. She'd refused to accept defeat. Mum vowed to fight on, alone if need be, like this was Dunkirk. The Blitz. In any case, Mum wasn't able to handle the war's loss with the degree of sportsmanship required. "It's all over," she said to me. Mum's face had been hollow with grief when the results of Rhodesia's first democratic election were announced over the radio. "You don't understand, Bobo. We've lost everything. Everything."

It's possible she lost her mind then too.

Or it's probable her mind had been lost for some time, but now the tide of war had gone out, and laid bare our insanity for all to see, or for it to be revealed. I mean, she was all of us, all of us Rhodesians; hurt, sore, surprised losers. She'd vowed to fight to the death; and even if everyone else had now forgotten that vow, she'd meant it.

"I'm not a coward, or a traitor," Mum had said.

The experiment of a Marxist socialist nation wasn't something she'd take lying down. So, though pregnant, her belly smacking against the pommel of her saddle, she fought with returning refugees; war-shocked ragbag groups of villagers making their way back home from Mozambique. On horseback she ran over the men beginning to clear the land above our dam. And she remained defiant when Zimbabwean soldiers, fresh recruits to a new nation from an old war, descended on the house and reminded us we'd already outstayed our welcome.

"No, we haven't," Mum said. "We were leaving anyway."

She wept bitterly in private; drank bravely in public.

"Your mother has difficulty cutting her losses," Dad had explained.

On the other hand, Dad excelled at cutting losses. He never looked back; he didn't keep score. He had to be told only once; he was ready to leave in a hurry when a place had become irreversibly unwelcoming, or when a place had become too tame, or too crowded. He moved us always to lands ever more remote and uncontested. And then those lands would fill up, or again become contested, and he'd move us again, and then again.

Dad had hired on for a season as a cattle manager on a remote ranch, miles from the last tiny dot on the map of southeast Zimbabwe; he wasn't being paid much, but our meat was free if he could shoot it. Also, although he was cattle manager, there were no cattle. Or there were thousands of cattle, but Dad had to find them first, and fence them in. "I needed a place to stall out for a year," Dad said afterward. "I needed to give us a chance to catch our breath. It seemed perfect, the ranch."

He thrived on movement.

Meantime, Mum hated transitions.

Transitions made her excitable, and excitability played up everything else that tended to go wrong with her. She had morning sickness and heart palpitations. Her fifth and final pregnancy was a difficult one, very trying. She'd endured weeks of bed rest at Mutare General, a lonely delivery, a painful recovery; and then the baby had died anyway, failure to thrive.

She was unsettled in her grief, the last of her lost children, a third child dead; her small pieces of comfort still in boxes on the veranda; her friends and family elsewhere. She was in no place to mother for a while. She wouldn't even look at the dogs, the faithful little pack we had back then; we'd never known her this bad. For weeks straight, she stared out the window of the little white ranch house.

As far as you could see in all directions the land tipped away from itself, like a vast low dome, shiny with heat. Acacia trees appeared like occasional calligraphy against the sky. It was beautiful, but there was little comfort there. When the generator came on for a few hours every evening, Mum played Roger Whittaker's "The Last Farewell" on the old 1970s record player, clicking the needle back and back and back.

She listened to that track until the vinyl warped.

She was haunted, anyone could tell, and there's no getting close to someone so haunted, there's no talking to someone who is so straining to hear the words of their dead, so tuned in for their dead's last song or final cry. She survived that haunting, though, in the end. In time, she broke away from her perpetual communion with the dead; she clicked onto a different sound track. "She always comes through," Dad had reassured us. "She'll be all right. You'll see."

MEANTIME, VANESSA AND I SPENT a lot of time in the back of a short-wheelbase Land Rover, out looking for cattle, lost. "I wasn't expecting hills here," Dad would say. "Not at all." Then he'd glance at the sun; its position relative to the horizon. "All right, if worse comes to worst, we'll follow it down, and see where it comes up in the morning."

Or he'd be a bit taken aback by the total lack of any hills in any direction, even standing on the roof of the Land Rover, still no hills, and the air thick and blue with dry-season smoke. "Anyone know where we are?" Dad would ask the team of fencers who'd hired on from remote villages in the area to work with him rounding up cattle gone feral during the war, and fencing them in.

"Chibodo couldn't speak their language either," Dad said of his chief tracker, a Manyika who'd followed him from the farm to the ranch out of curiosity more than anything. "So we just walked about looking for cattle, and the men put in fences when they felt like it, which wasn't very often because it was bloody hot and we were all getting paid peanuts."

White settlers had staked a claim on the ranch in the early 1920s. They shot most of the lions, all the wild dogs, and the Cape buffalo. After that they stocked the place with hardy cattle and then they went bush mad; one of them wrote a memoir about it, *My Life Was a Ranch*, not about going bush mad but about all the excitement leading up to that point.

"They did not go bush mad. You're making things up," Mum corrected me sharply. "And it's a very well written book. The way memoir should be done, in my opinion. It's filled with vivid, amusing anecdotes and interesting characters, sympathetically drawn."

"I know," I said. "I read it."

"Did you?" Mum pounced. "When? Do you remember? Do try to think. Because I loaned my copy to someone and I never got it back."

From the mid-1940s onward, the ranch had been left in the hands of a series of managers, bachelors who strived to be ideal Rhodesians just like the Brothers H. A lot of them went bush mad too. Then, during the war, whites abandoned the place altogether; soldiers and insurgents skirted it. It was too remote, too empty for battle.

The cattle went wild and the wildlife began to creep back onto the land. Kudu, their heads lifted above the tops of the thick, golden elephant grass, steadily curious. Herds of fat zebra, pythons the length of a Land Rover, jackals, elusive eland, groups of warthogs, impalas everywhere; a few leopards coughing their way through the kopjes.

"I love the farm I'm on the best," Dad said when I asked him which had been his favorite of all the lands he'd worked. "But I loved that ranch especially." Then he reflected for a moment. "Luckily I think I was too incompetent at the time to do too much damage to the place." He smiled happily at that thought. "Not often, but sometimes, it pays to be a bit useless, Bobo."

THE MIRACULOUS RANCH in southeast Zimbabwe was the wildest land we ever lived on, the least scarred. It wasn't a complete cure for what ailed, for the shocks and aftershocks of the war, and for all that had come with the war, but I think it was the beginning of the cure. Or the cure was ours for the metabolizing, if we knew it or not.

There weren't roads, it was unpredictable; we'd get set off course avoiding a downed tree or an area of quicksand; or a river would be too washed out to cross where we were expecting, and then we'd be lost. "Temporarily surprised by our destination would be the more diplomatic way to put it," Dad said, relishing it all.

He set up impromptu camps across the ranch, usually near a river for reference, if not for water. During the short wet season, the humid air was dense with insects; if it rained, the rivers churned red and swollen; we camped above the high-water mark in case of flash floods.

During the long dry season the veldt turned blond, the mopanes reached leafless grey branches into a bush-smoke yellow sky. We'd camp up against the riverbeds then, digging small wells, but also carrying water with us always, rationing water, noticing water, boiling water to make it safe for drinking.

Water and fire, there is no ground without them.

Dad had a khaki canvas safari tent; it had holes in the roof and rips in the floor, it leaked insects, but it could accommodate a camping cot, a stool, a trunk, and a paraffin lamp. Dad had hung a small mirror on the front tent pole, and he shaved there; the scrape-scrape of his razor mixing with the cool call of emerald-spotted doves at dawn, the turpentine scent of the mopane logs in the fire heating water for tea.

Vanessa and I shared a little orange-and-blue tent, also canvas, but sun-rotted and bent. It smelled as if feverish children had vomited in it, which we had. We had ancient camp cots; their rusty metal legs sagged and teetered when we turned over. We learned to sleep very still, the way you sleep in boarding school, as if dead, so as not to excite the attention of the matrons.

Mostly, we stayed in camp while Dad and the men searched for feral cattle or fenced the sky or tilted at the sun. The days were long, hot. We dozed in the shade, dug tiny boreholes in the dry riverbeds; I arranged impromptu concerts for Vanessa. At night we sat around two fires; the four of us outsiders quietly around a small fire, the dozen or so local fencers noisily around a big fire.

Dad didn't say much beyond what was necessary. Cephas Chibodo only made noises to the fire, as he tended it, "Eh, ehhhh," he'd say, turning a log a little, coaxing an ember into flame. Vanessa and I didn't talk much either. There wasn't much to say. We were here; the sky turned above us; the air was solid with insects and frogs chorusing. Beneath us, the ground surrendered the day's heat. Water in the kettle popped and hissed.

We went to sleep not long after dark.

Then we'd hear Dad shouting before dawn. "Chibodo! Moto! Fuga moto!" And we'd hear Cephas Chibodo making a fire. The kettle would begin its song again. "Right!" Dad would be giving marching orders; our tent would get a shake. "Rise and shine!"

One foot in front of the other, he and Cephas Chibodo walked back and forth across that enormous tract of wild ranch. They dead-reckoned fence lines, miles at a time. Sometimes the fencers came behind, slowly, with metal posts, shovels, and hammers; it was heavy work.

They made a sound like gunshots, hammers on those posts.

Ka-pow, ka-pow, ka-pow.

Then they tracked cattle. Some days Vanessa and I were allowed to tag along. On those days, we lost ourselves, or found ourselves, in my father's and Cephas Chibodo's wake. They walked quickly, eyes lifted to the clouds of dust ahead of us; the cattle were wily and bush-savvy, but they kicked up a storm. "Three miles an hour will keep you in business," Dad told us, if we'd begged to come along.

I learned—or, I really understood—what three miles an hour felt like in my body; I had to run to keep up. I didn't bother to swat away the flies; I stopped asking if anyone knew where we were. Walking was serious business, and Dad and Cephas Chibodo walked for hours at a time. The goal was to cover ground and find cattle, not to stop and admire the view.

Admiring the view was for when you were lost; when you were lost, you could breathe a bit, take stock. Being lost put Dad at ease; it froze his perpetual motion. He'd be propped up against a tree, a cigarette between his lips. Someone would have built a fire; the kettle would be on to boil. Dad had looked peaceful then, eyes half shut against the sun, smiling a little; surveying the swell or the swoop or the skim of the land, comparing it to where we'd just come from. "That was the wildest place we ever lived, Bobo. You could really fall off the map out there."

DAD HAD ALWAYS BEEN GOOD WITH MAPS, in theory. He'd been the navigator in a rally in East Africa a couple of times; although I don't think he ever made it to the finish. "That sticky black cotton soil in a Ford Anglia; the worst roads in the *world*," Mum said in his defense. "Most of the cars sank to their sumps two miles from the starting flag. The East Africa Rally's not just Formula One, you know, round and round, no chance of getting lost."

Anyway, it's not possible to learn the lay of the land from paper, or in a car, and especially not in a car sunk to its sump. You have to learn it with your feet. So although Dad could trace topographical maps in his head, and translate what he saw into hills and ridges and valleys, it took time for him to put that realization into his body.

When Dad first came to East and southern Africa he'd wildly underestimate distances, or he'd miscalculate the ruggedness of the terrain; he'd be taken by surprise, the beautiful ferocity of it all. It took a few years for the smallness of England to wear off, for the rigidity of his education to melt, for the sheer vast scale of southern Africa to register; it was bigger even than his dreams of it during his sad, cold, lonely British childhood.

"It was a miserable house," he said of those early years with his ill-matched parents. "So as soon as I could, I walked out of it; a garden, a backyard, a stable, hedgerows. Inside, I could never tell which was what and who was who. But outside, things made sense. Things that were supposed to sting stung. Things that were supposed to bite bit."

By the age of seven—showing a precocious talent for planning well ahead, a talent not necessarily exercised through the remainder of his life—Dad had already calculated his only sensible option. "I informed my nanny," he said, "as soon as I'd fulfilled my childhood obligations, I'd bugger off to Africa."

Noo, he called his nanny; she'd raised him from birth, the sober, stern, nurturing witness to his childhood. To show the seriousness of his intentions, he drew her a picture of a giraffe, and on the back of the picture, in a considered hand, my father announced he expected he'd be leaving by the first possible boat in about eleven years for either Cape Town or Mombasa. He showed her both places on the globe in the nursery.

"What a good idea," Noo agreed.

She helpfully prepared Dad for this certain future by taking him on little rambles on the South Downs, pointing out birds and rabbits.

"She made sure I knew the difference between a wren and a chaffinch, the difference between a coal tit and a blue tit; all their songs. We collected their eggs; she showed me a cuckoo chick in a dunnock nest. I learned all that from her. She really tried. We tromped miles and miles through the mud together, Noo always in her great white nurse's cape; it scared up the pheasants."

Still, it really wasn't enough; hedgehogs, badgers, water rats, the rare otter, it was barely toothy enough for a Beatrix Potter storybook, let alone for a soul-wounded, red-blooded child. As far as my father could see, the only cure for what ailed him was the opportunity to become irredeemably lost, and that was a rare treat in 1950s England. Also, there was almost zero opportunity to be killed by a predator on a casual afternoon outing.

Dad loved old maps for the promise of spaces still filled with wilderness, for places unmarked by the crosshatch of development, for the possibility of land without roads. It didn't occur to him at the time that it wasn't endless. "I saw the last of the best of it, Bobo," he told me years later. "I'm glad I didn't realize at the time."

Gone so quickly; over so fast.

Mum, raised in western Kenya and steeped in the glory of empire, loved old maps too. Compulsively nostalgic, and a hoarder by nature, she keeps old atlases on a special bookshelf. She refers to them during the BBC's news and culture radio shows; they're her friends, like her pets.

"Now let me see, Azerbaijan. Ah, well, back when this atlas was published, it wasn't even a separate country. It was just a bit of purple bubble gum stuck on the western heel of the Soviet Socialist Republic's hobnail boot." Mum would offer this information smugly. "This atlas is quite old," Mum would say. "Quite old," she'd repeat, approvingly running her hands over the pages.

She likes atlases in which it's still the cold war, but she adores leafing through atlases in which Iran is still Persia, Zimbabwe is still Southern Rhodesia, Botswana is still Bechuanaland, and Sri Lanka is still Ceylon. Her fascination is in a world that has existed chiefly in the imagination; a place of heat, denial, nostalgia, and juleps.

"I find great comfort there," Mum says. "In those lovely old stories of people going to far-flung parts of the empire. They were always racked with fever. They were forced to drink like fish. They had to make it up-country during the monsoon season."

So when Mum refers to "going up-country," although she has the empire in her head, India specifically, she means something entirely different. She means driving from the hot, low Zambezi Valley where the farm is, up the Muchinga Escarpment to the place my mother calls Alcatraz—the little cottage Vanessa and Rich built for my parents near the Rock.

Both Alcatraz and the Rock are perched on the summit of a small, glorious kopje near the Kafue River. The verandas of both places overlook the hills surrounding the little river town of Kafue. Kafue, with its old blue-and-white colonial-era police station, its green mosque, its gabled storefronts and buzzing open-air markets.

It's beautiful up there, there are wild forests, birds tumble through the sky, at sunset the light pulses in the west; it's a whole show. And at dawn again, the light emerges from the east as if it has been dunked in the vivid blue Kafue River overnight and rinsed iridescent. It's also much cooler on the plateau than in the valley; the rains are more predictable, it's lusher; there are no tsetse flies, you can keep horses and cattle.

However, no one else in Zambia refers to the plateau where Alcatraz and the Rock are built as up-country, they wouldn't understand the reference, and my mother knows this, but she doesn't care. If she has to be the lone representative of gentility in a country of pleasant but otherwise basic fellow citizens, she'll do it. So, up-country, she insists, thereby making sly literary and geographical reference to Simla, the summer escape for the British imperialists in India from the feverish sweatboxes of Bombay and Calcutta.

Mum has reread the Raj Quartet, *The Far Pavilions*, and *Kim* many times, and has longed to go to India her entire life. Like my father and the maps of Africa he'd pored over as a child, Mum pored over maps of the Indian subcontinent. She pictured herself drinking chai on the little blue train that wends through the mountains from Siliguri to Darjeeling. She wanted to go to all the fabulous markets in Delhi—saris, carpets, curry powder. She wanted to meet an Indian prince, she wanted to ride an elephant, and she wanted to try hashish.

"Like in one of Graham Greene's novels," Mum said. "Or, even better, Somerset Maugham. You know the stories. There's always a cholera outbreak and someone getting murdered on a rubber plantation; it's unbearably muggy."

She knew she'd probably never go to India and lie in a bemused stupor on a pile of lavish carpets in the high desert, sharing a pipe with camel drivers—that century had slipped by—but the entertainment she derived from imagining that she might one day still sail out to the "Jewel in the Crown" kept her from longing too much for other things she also couldn't have, or would never do.

My parents matched each other perfectly in this regard. It was a lucky coincidence; not many people would have survived what they put each other through.

"YOUR PARENTS WERE SO RECKLESS." I am told this often.

And sometimes they were reckless; it was fun for them, and often for us. We'd end up in a story. But we'd also end up in a story because of nothing reckless at all; simply the way a life fully led will take you out of your way and beyond your control.

Tracking a zebra once on the ranch, it had happened; we were lost two whole days. It should have been a fairly easy early-morning outing. It should have been a heart shot at dawn. But at the last moment, the zebra snapped back against something, perhaps a tsetse-fly bite. The creature startled into a crippled trot. Dad swore, threw his rifle across the seat.

"Hold tight," he shouted, and we were off.

Vanessa and I sat in the back of the Land Rover, flattened against the glass dividing us from the front seats, our eyes closed; the Land Rover lashed with mopane branches until the air was filled with the scent of turpentine. Dad smoked cigarette after cigarette, and occasionally shouted to Cephas Chibodo, "Do you see anything?"

And Cephas Chibodo's reassuring, "Eh, eh," guiding us through the mopane woodland after the animal. He deftly spider-crawled his way around the vehicle, sometimes collapsing completely backward, or folding himself down the windscreen, to avoid getting whipped off the roof altogether. Then the woodland got too dense, even for Cephas Chibodo's prodigious ability to hang on.

Dad turned off the engine then.

We'd been going all day, high revs in thick sand a lot of the time; we'd burned one jerry can of spare diesel already. There were seven people total; three local villagers brought along to butcher the animal, two kids brought along to give their mother a break, and one Manyika tracker.

We had water enough for the rest of the day and the night; we could always make fire; there were two paraffin lamps. No one was going to starve to death or die of exposure. The mosquitoes weren't too bad. At worst, some of us might be very thirsty in about sixteen hours.

Dad lit another cigarette.

"Okay." He'd made up his mind. He turned to Vanessa and me. "Sit tight," he said. "When you hear a shot, I'll be back in the same amount of time I was gone, in reverse."

Dad packed a flask of brandy, cigarettes, bullets. Cephas Chibodo brought tobacco and newspaper to roll it in. They both checked their pockets for matches. Then without saying anything they took off together into the mopane thicket, moving very fast, unhesitatingly.

In that blunting hot low veldt light, they appeared not as people, but as shapes. First they were dark patterns against the trees, then they were shadows between the trees, and then they were gone. After that, there was nothing to show that they'd been, except a few scuffle marks on the ground. Also the buzz of their absence; after a while, though, even that burned off.

Meantime, the earth between the trees was the same glittering, white sugary sand over cracked, dark brown clay in every direction. There was little to distinguish the east from the west; the woodland obscured the sky, everything very bright, very yellow. Vanessa and I dozed, took refuge from the heat.

The three local villagers smoked and watched the sun; they talked and slept. When the sun clipped the top of the trees to the west, the villagers strung up a tarpaulin and lit the two paraffin lamps. Then all of a sudden, the light dropped, the way it does in southern Africa, everything turned magenta, orange, a riot of violet and pink, then just as suddenly dark.

There's no gentle dusk, no nautical twilight, no soft evening. You're either ready for it, or not. One moment the sky is suffused with a vivid pulsing sunset, it looks as if it'll go on forever; and the next moment it's a black and moonless sky, sword-pierced through with stars.

Nothing prepares you for the sudden darkness of a southern African night, even if you've never known anything else. It's always as if the light had been smothered rather than gently slid behind the horizon. But it prepares you for certain endings, such a leap from painted skies to night.

By which I mean definite endings.

Sudden endings.

VANESSA AND I, waiting with the laborers around a fire, heard the shot just after dark. It took Dad, Cephas Chibodo, and the rest of the men until dawn to skin and butcher the young stallion. For a long time we ate fresh zebra hung from the meat safe on the veranda; and for a long time after that we ate dried zebra. It tasted metallic, killed too late in the day after too much stress.

But the zebra's magnificent hide—mesmerizing, and perfect, an argument in favor of the existence of God—lay in front of the fireplace on the sitting room floor, until the legs rotted through with too many rainy seasons, and until Mum's dogs chewed off most of the stripes. "Like everything else," Mum sighed.

It's all always been about loss in our family, an abundance of loss. Although some things were surprisingly tenacious or were grimly hoarded. Books, of course, thermos flasks, and Mum's orange Le Creuset pots; a little Buddha statue she'd stolen. We took only what could fit in a short-wheelbase Land Rover. It wasn't much once the saddles and all the dogs were loaded up.

But my father seemed to have surrendered to loss, to have welcomed the opportunity to leave it all behind again. It must have taken some undoing, although it helped that he'd chosen to live where a title deed wasn't a guarantee to land; a gun wasn't a guarantee of life. "The only guarantee is you'll end up losing it all anyway," Dad had said.

He sounded positively cheered by this certain outcome.

It matched the experience of his life.

It affirmed his decision to pare down and down and down until he was needless, invincible, he walked alone. Or he walked with Harry, the two of them sharing the jaunty statesmanship of creatures near the zenith of fulfilling their contracts with the universe.

Harry was doing what he'd come to do; and my father had done the same. He'd been born with a tarnished spoon in his mouth, and he'd spent his life trying to lose the taste. He'd nearly overshot the goal. Loss and getting lost, losing, they're underappreciated accomplishments.

"Tim Fuller went to Africa and lost everything," the aunts had lamented.

And in every important way they were correct.

My father had gone to Africa and he'd lost *nearly* everything. He'd lost nearly everything, but it hadn't been easy.

CHAPTER FIVE

Don't Just Stand There, Do Something

For a dozen strange days, I'd divided myself, hours with Dad, hours with Mum. Hours and hours, it had seemed a peculiar concentration of parenthood all of a sudden. I hadn't been accustomed to Mum and Dad undiluted.

Mum had been stuck in front of the television racked with coughing fits for much of our stay, too ill and distracted to enjoy the novels she'd brought for her holidays, historical fiction about the British royal family. "I've lost my concentration and I can't keep track of all the trickery," she'd complained. "All the beheadings and bastardry."

She'd watched many BBC productions of soothing murders, but as things had become more arduous for us, she'd turned for comfort to an obscure Eastern European sports channel whose budget apparently stretched to race walking and marathons, but not much further. "It does me good to watch other people suffer pointlessly of their own accord. It makes my involuntary suffering seem less futile," Mum had explained. She knew how to cope; they both did, my parents.

You notice these obvious things too old, too late.

Too late, I'd soaked up my hours with Mum; I'd soaked up my hours with Dad. I'd known these two people well, but I'd never known them intimately. When we were children, they seemed mostly preoccupied with their own dense worlds. They weren't nurturing types; they let us tag along, they didn't let us in.

"The sensible child-rearing books I read insisted children be allowed to foster a robust sense of independence," Mum had said. She'd left Vanessa in a pram to stare into the leaves of a tree at the bottom of the garden and she'd relinquished me to the care of a goat. "Horace wasn't housebroken, but he was very maternal," Mum had assured me.

By this simple method, my parents had attempted to raise a couple of resilient daughters; they'd expected us to stomach a little disorder, to handle a few surprises here and there. "Keep buggering on." We'd taken that phrase straight from Winston Churchill, or Dad had, and then we'd all started using it.

"KBO," Rich signed off his letters and emails.

If the Fullers had a code it was that; if we'd had a coat of arms, it would have shown two rampant dogs, a shovel, and a gun. Our motto would have been along the lines of *"In Vino, Invictus."** We'd have lauded qualities of loyalty, heroism, and reverent irreverence.

And in the hours after Dad's death, Mum and I had lived up to the code of the Fullers. We'd been dogged and brave and true, buggering on soberly and sadly through the hordes of refugees, Mum wheezing. We'd decided our first stop should be the British Embassy, where it turned out nothing we said mattered because "the

---

* In wine, undefeated.

gentleman in question had opted to reside abroad for the last fifty years."

"He was still English," Mum had argued. She'd refrained from bringing up the matter of Dad's familial connection to the Crown Jewels and Queen Victoria, also polo with princes and shooting tigers in India with royalty, but I could tell it had cost her. "Living in Africa didn't turn him into a *Zambian*," Mum had said.

"Possibly not," the woman from the embassy had agreed doubtfully. "But unfortunately British entitlements would have run out six months after the gentleman in question decided to leave the United Kingdom." Mum and I had turned down the proffered cups of tea, and had left the embassy confirmed in our prejudice against the English.

"The poor queen. It used to *mean* something to be British," Mum said. "I feel quite shaken. *'The gentleman in question.'* What an irritating phrase." She riffled around in her handbag, unearthed her anti-mad pills, and swallowed a couple. "In our day, one was expected to live abroad; it was the done thing. Wasn't that the whole point of the bloody empire?" Mum sniffed unhappily. "Or I guess more my parents' generation, they were expected to live abroad and keep the map pink, and even they lost India."

I found a café with internet so we could regroup and plan our immediate future. For her part, Mum intended to rebuff her next invitation from the British High Commission in Lusaka to one of their Awful Dos for expats. "Warm white wine and crusty bits of liver pâté," she said. "What's the point of enduring all those dreary speeches and limp handshakes if they then won't help you out in a crisis abroad?"

Meantime, I made arrangements for the cremation of Dad's body. Or I believed I was making the arrangements for the cremation of Dad's body, but Mum had been quite correct. It wasn't as easy as it looked having an emergency in a foreign language; it was like high-stakes performance art. It was mostly guesswork, to be honest.

"What did I tell you?" Mum said. "People always accuse me of exaggerating and making things up. I never do."

We arrived at the funeral home—I'd found it online; it had appeared to be a short walk from the café; it was not—sweating, red-faced, and Mum had to keep taking urgent hauls off her asthma puffer. We accepted the offers of water, and drank it like speed walkers.

"I can't stay here a minute longer than absolutely necessary," Mum had insisted as we'd slogged our way across the city.

In the funeral home lobby we spoke loudly and in chorus, we drew pictures, we mimed. We flapped our arms to indicate we had an urgent flight to catch and therefore we needed Dad's corpse in, and his ashes out, of the facility as quickly as possible. We were ready to buy an urn, transfer cash, and sign all waivers on the spot.

Our haste was unseemly by almost any standards. It began to feel, even to us, more as if we'd committed murder than suffered bereavement. "Oh, dear," Mum said. "I know we must look heartless to you. But really, we're not. It's simply that I live in central Africa and my daughter's an American. We're accustomed to horror."

The funeral director hurried us out of the reception area through to another room in which there were shelves and shelves of urns, a few coffins. Mum eschewed crystal, mahogany, and porcelain for an affordable tin roughly the shape and size of a small bomb casing. "But how will we know if they're actually Dad's ashes in here?" she asked, shaking it as if to make sure it wasn't already occupied.

"Oh, Mum!"

Mum flashed one of her terrifying smiles at the funeral director, but she was directing her comments at me. "Never mind, Bobo. I'm sure it's all perfectly fine. I'm sure we'll get Dad's ashes back in this tin, and not the ashes of some nameless Hungarian."

"Of course we will," I said.

"Or some unfortunate refugee," Mum added. She implied air quotes around the word "refugee." There was no air-conditioning; a fan stirred the muggy air around. "All right," Mum said, mopping her brow. "Put my husband in here, please." She tapped the bomb casing and directed a final terrifying smile at the funeral director. "*Köszönöm* very much indeed," she said. "You've been very helpful, most accommodating, terribly kind."

WE GOT BACK TO THE HOTEL in the late afternoon, exhausted from it all; Dad's death, tromping around the hot city in a refugee crisis. "One down, two to go," Mum said. She put up her feet on the bed, took another anti-mad pill, and poured herself a well-earned brandy, dash of water, some ice. Meantime, I spent a few hours on the phone with unsympathetic airline officials. "You are *much* bossier than I," Mum had reasoned. "You should do it, it's easy for you."

I managed—after the kind of phone athletics that confirms it hasn't been worth the exchange of simplicity for convenience—to secure two air tickets from Budapest to Lusaka via London and Johannesburg; I also negotiated the partial refund of a dead man's air ticket along the same unlikely route; but I was having some trouble securing permission to have Dad's ashes on board with us.

The Ethiopians were fine; the South Africans didn't mind. The British and Germans seemed worried, though. They asked many questions, they put me on hold for fifteen minutes at a time, managers were sought. "Good thing we're not Jewish, tell them." Mum waved her glass at me; the ice clunked. "Or we'd have to bring the whole corpse in a tachrichim." She seemed proud of knowing this word, and she repeated it a few times, attempting various pronunciations. "Do you think it's a hard 'cheem' or more like you're clearing your throat 'gheeem'?"

I put my hand over the receiver. "Mum!"

Mum shrugged innocently and took a sip of her drink. "Just trying to help," she said. "It's lucky you're so naturally bossy, Bobo." She smiled encouragingly. "Tell them he's in a very neat box." She assessed the box. "They haven't lost the knack of getting rid of a body quickly and efficiently around here. It's much smaller than anything I usually try to wrestle on board as hand luggage," she admitted.

Dad's cremated remains weighed a little less than three kilograms minus the bomb casing and the cardboard box. "Seven pounds," Mum said. She can do these conversions in her head, I can't. I had to tell the airline agents my father's exact dead weight, it was the same as his birth weight. I cried, huge unexpected tears at that realization, but Mum remained dry-eyed for the moment, her natural suspicion overriding any lurking sentimentality. "You do think it's all of Dad?" she asked.

"Yes, Mum," I said, drying my eyes. "I do."

"Not even three kilograms," Mum said. "I do think that's very average." She sighed philosophically, her shoulders sagging. "Oh, dear, it doesn't amount to much in the end, does it?"

"No," I said.

Then we sat with the box between us on Mum's bed, silently and intolerably sad. We took one of her emergency happy pills. We agreed they were useless; we felt shocked and despondent to the core. "Probably find they're a useless batch," Mum said, shaking the pill bottle. "You can never tell with my Indian chemist. Sometimes your head goes off like a bomb, sometimes nothing at all."

Neither of us felt like supper; I made us each a cup of sweet, milky tea. We both agreed we shouldn't cry; it would only make us feel worse, although neither of us could imagine what would make us feel better. We'd hit a looming, terrible, stalled-out sense that we wouldn't be able to go on without Dad telling us what to do next.

"What now?" Mum asked.

I didn't know what now. I knew what next, but I didn't know what now. And I hadn't realized until that very moment that "next" and "now" were, of course, two entirely different things. The future is easier to worry about; the present is harder to do. Also, I couldn't imagine the present; but I could imagine the future, mostly.

If all went well, or at least if things didn't go any worse, we'd be leaving Budapest at five in the morning, flying to Hamburg, and from there to Heathrow. Two days after that, we'd be flying back to Zambia via South Africa. But I couldn't quite patch together in my mind how I'd get all of us from here to there and from there to Chirundu, and from Chirundu to the farm.

"Don't just stand there," Dad had always said. "Do something."

During moments of difficulty, Dad was a big believer in casting caution to the wind. The worse things got, the more likely he was to throw his shoulders back and go over the top. I suppose it was all that early exposure to Winston Churchill, Rupert Brooke, and Rudyard Kipling; those hymns, "When I Survey the Wondrous Cross." No wonder boarding-school-educated Brits were such easy targets in foreign wars.

I swung my legs off the side of the bed. "We should pack," I said. "For a start."

"Oh, Bobo," Mum said. "How clever of you. What a good idea." She wilted under the covers as if suddenly deboned. "But it's just hitting me," she said. "I can't pack all this lot up. Not without help. Not ever."

She looked around the room, feebly uncertain, as if someone else had been camping there for two weeks. "Dad usually does the packing," she said. And suddenly I saw their marriage, not as I'd seen it until now, a rollicking grand misadventure set in East and southern Africa, romance, racism, and tragedy, but as they must have felt it, a comforting habit, worn into grooves and creases over the decades. In all the uncertainty they'd courted, through all their little victories and their grand losses, they'd been each other's constant.

"We're like a pair of geese," Dad had once said. "Mated for life."

And improbably they'd met somehow, somewhere in the middle of all that life. They'd meted out the costs and the benefits; they'd worked out how to work it out. They'd leaned into each other's strengths, shored up each other's weaknesses; delighted in each other's foibles; tolerated each other's addictions; respected each other's opinions.

"Tub," Dad might say. "How about we put in a patch of elephant grass this side of plot one? You know, by the dambo?"

"Mm, and it's a pull crop too," Mum might reply. "Sound idea."

My favorite childhood nights were when I went to sleep with a heap of dogs snoring on my bed, and my parents murmuring about farming on the veranda. They spoke softly and quickly then, the way people do when they've developed a code; the tone was the quieting assurance of escalating agreement—nurseries, nitrogen, pH levels, beneficial microbes, nematodes, suckers, loam, lime, breeding, flowering, fruiting.

"Divide, conquer, and delegate," Dad always counseled.

Mum ran the household, organized meals, took care of the pets. She treated the sick and tended the maimed; a line of patients greeted her every morning as she emerged from breakfast. She was in charge of livestock, poultry, orchards, and fish. Soil conservation, and the flower and vegetable gardens; these were also her purview. She did the careful work, the weighing and measuring, the husbandry. She was the better farmer of the two.

Dad was the visionary and by the end he'd perfected the art.

He'd have his grand ideas before dawn, he'd describe them by breakfast, and then he'd dash down to the pub for his eleven-o'clock brandy, leaving other people to do the work. Meantime, he shot rabid dogs and venomous snakes as needed; he did the farm shopping, he made a balls-up of the accounts, and he undertook to do the packing. He was the better organizer of the two.

It was an art perfected over a lifetime to get our farm shopping balanced in the back of a pickup. There'd be food, of course, irrigation piping always; usually a repaired generator, or an engine leaking oil; fish food, fertilizer, and usually at least one miserable dog returning from a humiliating visit to the vet.

I couldn't imagine Mum packing her own suitcase.

"I'll do it," I said.

Mum sniffed. "Oh, thank you, Bobo," she said.

There had been problems with Customs and Immigration before, not least because Mum breaks into a guilty sweat the moment she's confronted with uniformed airline officials. She blames hostile border crossings in central Africa, "the socialist banana republics," she says, darkly. "They do an absolute strip search every chance they get." But she also breaks into a sweat because she's a compulsive smuggler. "Dad was always very good at finding secret hiding places for my few bits of comforting contraband."

"I think we're going to have to leave your interesting collection," I said. "We've got enough to explain to the authorities as it is. And you have no room."

I turned on the television. It was still tuned to the strange Eastern European channel Mum had found to replace the BBC's soothing murders. Another marathon was on; a rerun surely, there couldn't be this many marathons going on all the time anywhere on Earth.

"Maybe just a couple of beer mats," Mum pleaded, watching me throw out a block of partially consumed pink Hungarian cheese spread, cracking at the edges. I put a single beer mat into her suitcase. Mum's attention flitted fretfully between the television and my packing. "Oh, Bobo, you're so sensible."

I folded up the last of Mum's clothes, leaving out her black trousers and her red silk shirt for the morning. There were three bags of rubbish surrounding the dustbin now, but Mum's suitcase zipped, effortlessly and neatly. It was easy to lift.

"Very clever of you, Bobo," Mum said.

"It's late," I said. "Why don't you get ready for bed?"

Mum obediently got up, bathed, and brushed her teeth.

Meantime, I packed Dad's small leather duffel. Two cotton hankies, one pair of posh trousers, two button-down shirts, a navy blue sweater, three pairs of cotton boxer shorts, a pair of handmade leather shoes from Thailand, four pairs of socks, a spare pipe, two tins of tobacco, one Ian Fleming novel, half read.

"Oh, Bobo," Mum said, padding behind me and climbing back into bed; she was pink from the bath. She smiled bravely, her eyes settling on Dad's duffel. "*Casino Royale* will forever have a special place in our library," she said; she seized the throat of her night-gown. "A sacred spot," Mum continued. "I'll smother it in Blue Death to keep the silverfish and the termites out."

"Should I leave on the television?" I asked.

Mum shook her head; "No, no, Bobo."

"How about the bathroom light?"

Mum shook her head again. "No, no, no. No need to waste the electricity. I'll be okay." She smiled sweetly.

It reminded me of putting a small child to bed, alone for the first time. On hotel stationery, I wrote down the number of my room as a reminder.

"Call if you need anything," I said.

Mum nodded.

"The taxi comes at five," I reminded her.

"Blue Death to bedbugs," Mum said bravely.

"Blue Death," I replied.

Mum closed her eyes obediently. It felt cruel to leave her, al-though the only thing she'd have hated more than being alone would have been me crawling into bed with her, holding her close. That would have been a very American thing to do. She'd have stiffened to concrete on contact. I turned off the lights and let my-self out of Mum's room, the first whole night without Dad.

"No, no," Mum said, as if she'd read my mind, as she so often does, correctly usually. "No, no," she repeated, her voice so faint and reedy she seemed already asleep, or speaking from another realm. "He's right here with me. Dad's by my side. I'm not alone, Bobo. Don't worry. He's all around me. I can feel him. I'll be fine. I'll be perfectly, perfectly fine."

CHAPTER SIX

If You Are It, You Don't Need to Say It

Vanessa's stint at the clinic in KwaZulu-Natal had reversed her circadian rhythms, apparently. She couldn't sleep at night, and had to sleep instead for much of the day. In any case, she no longer kept traditional hours.

"Whatever else is wrong with Vanessa," Mum had said when it was too late and Vanessa was already doing group, "she certainly doesn't need a drying-up stint."

"I think it's drying out," I'd said. "Not drying up."

"Oh?" Mum had feigned surprised. "Is it?"

But even Mum couldn't deny that the initial results of Vanessa's drying-up stint had been spectacular. She'd swept onto the veranda at the Rock, backlit against a brilliant April sun the day of her release from the clinic in KwaZulu-Natal, eighteen months before Dad had ended up in Budapest; her blond hair freshly washed, her eyes bright. All the oxygen in a three-mile-square area had rushed to greet her. She was the lyric to any number of songs.

"It was just like boarding school except no one was allowed a razor," Vanessa had reported, sitting behind the bar, from where she could more easily hold court. She had the Persians on her lap, two of them, Puss Catastrophe and Puss Catapult; Rich had picked their names.

We'd all been agog about the clinic.

Or I'd been agog.

The moment preliminary greetings had been completed Rich had declared his immediate intention to go into the office. "Tycoon magnate time," he'd said, chain-smoking his way out of the conversation. Dad had patted Vanessa on the shoulder. "I'll get Mum to tell me all about it later," he'd lied, and had fled for Lusaka. "Farm shopping," he'd explained.

The veranda door had closed with a bang.

Mum had glared after them, her expression one of sour envy: "Why I am always left with the boring jobs?"

"An alcoholic stole the cleaning fluid out of the broom cupboard," Vanessa had continued, persisting with her enthusiastic endorsement of her experience at the KwaZulu-Natal clinic, even with half her audience gone and half the remaining audience in a state of hostile detachment.

"Whyever would someone do that?" Mum had asked. She'd begun cleaning her fingernails on the edge of a beer mat.

Vanessa had bravely soldiered on with her account. "And a kleptomaniac stole my knickers off the washing line," she'd said. "It was hilarious."

Mum had looked at her watch and had sighed audibly.

"Anyway I'm going to have to be very boring from now on," Vanessa had said firmly. "There will be no more 'Olé, I am a bandit' for me, no more 'Let's have a party.'"

With that, Mum had clambered off her barstool, stiffly but with dignity. "Well, you didn't get that attitude from my side of the family," she'd said. And then, as if Vanessa had suddenly vanished from the Rock, and as if this were the first time I'd heard of it, Mum had turned to me conspiratorially. "Boofy had funny tendencies, poor thing. Dad's mother, you know. I met her just the once when I was pregnant with Vanessa; she died shortly after that. Boofy, I mean. Not Vanessa, obviously. She was what used to be called a dipsomaniac."

Mum had strung the declaration out—dip-so-maniac—as if the word "alcoholic" didn't yet exist, as if we'd no need for it in our modern times. "And one or two of Boofy's sisters were serious tipplers too; your paternal great-aunts, gin at breakfast, that sort of thing," Mum had said. "I believe, a couple of them anyway."

"I know," I'd said. "You've already told me."

Mum had glared as if I too were headed down the same road as either Vanessa or Boofy; nowhere good in any case. "Oh, what's the point? I'm going to put my feet up in Alcatraz with a nice little dog. I'll ask Nixon for tea. Don't bother to move if you don't have to, either of you."

Then Vanessa and I had watched Mum as she'd marched with tiny, fiery determination down the little stretch of steep, rocky red road from the Rock to Alcatraz with Paddy, one of Vanessa's nice little dogs, tucked under her arm. After a while, we'd heard the BBC World News shouting from the veranda at Alcatraz. Then there was the clatter of Mr. Nixon ferrying tea down to Mum.

We'd pictured the performance: Paddy being momentarily displaced to make room for the tea, Mr. Nixon pouring the first cup for Mum; Paddy being returned to his rightful spot. Mum thanking Mr. Nixon extravagantly, "Oh, zekomo, Nixon. Zekomo kwambili." And then we knew Mr. Nixon would be taking his leave backward, bowing and scraping his way out of Alcatraz, ironically surely.

Vanessa and I had watched as he'd slogged up the steep little stretch of red road to the Rock with the empty tea tray. Dogs and cats had threaded around his ankles and jumped up on him. He'd conversed with them amiably. Mum liked Mr. Nixon because he bowed and scraped. Also, he didn't kick Vanessa's dogs and cats like the rest of us.

"She'll outlive Dad," Vanessa had predicted at last.

The kitchen door had slammed shut behind Mr. Nixon and everything had settled down again; the dogs had curled up in their dusty nests, a thousand cats had rubbed back and forth against the closed kitchen door, a sprinkler had flicked diamonds at an emerald lawn.

"It won't be easy," Vanessa had said. We'd both sat for a while in the terror of that truth. It was hard to imagine either of our parents gone, let alone one without the other. She was half his world. He was half hers.

She'll sink without him, I'd thought.

She'll dissolve.

"She'll go straight over the falls," I'd said.

"Or," Vanessa said, lighting a cigarette, "she'll be fine." Vanessa exhaled authoritatively. "Watch, Al-Bo. If poor Dad goes first, she'll be absolutely fine. She'll probably be the last man standing. Bindi says people like Mum live forever."

So then we'd both sat for a while in the terror of that truth.

MUM'S DIFFICULT TO HANDLE, overbred and underschooled. She's never taken orders from anyone, she wasn't going to start listening to her two daughters this late in the game. The only person she'd ever listened to was Dad, and this was partly because he never told her to do anything. "Well done, Tub," he'd say. "You wore this old goat out." Or, "What do you say we take this show on the road?" Or, "Where's my other half?"

Mum had survived a woman's worst bereavement, not once but three times, and she hadn't let it destroy her. She'd come back each time, twice as curious about everything; also twice as alive and twice as impossible. She isn't consumed by life, the way my father was; instead she devours it herself, she is the consumer. Sampling everything life has to offer, but deliciously, and slowly and methodically.

Unless with company, my father ate as if half expecting his meal to bite back; a preemptive strike against whatever was on his plate. On the other hand, Mum took all night to peck her way through the tiniest portion. "I can eat only a very little at a time," she always said. "I must be very careful not to overdo it. I have a delicate constitution."

She had the farm carpenter make special bookstands; I have one too. Mum keeps one by her plate, it's the way she was raised on the Uasin Gishu plateau. Everyone reading at table, everyone feeding half their supper to the dogs.

"Ours was a very warm, very happy childhood," she always says.

"Total bloody chaos," Dad had agreed. "The only way there was any control was if the old man brought out his shotgun and put a few slugs through the ceiling. That usually got some attention."

But the rest of the time, Mum and her wild sister, Glennis, did what they liked. Which was to drink homemade wine, and read their way through piles of books, and to be with dogs, and horses, and to dance at the club with British soldiers sent out from the UK to quell the Mau Mau. Once a week they went to the cinema, and once a year to the Convent School Pantomime, starring members of the community. "My father always went as Old Mother Riley,"

Mum said. "Until the nuns put a stop to it. There were complaints about his bloomers from some of the infys."

An infy is what Mum calls anyone who isn't superior. We both stole that from V. S. Naipaul; she's read his entire oeuvre, of course. Also all of Paul Theroux, she adores his long, grumpy travelogues, his trips around Africa especially. "Angola was the last straw," she reported. "It was so ghastly, Paul Theroux wrote off the whole of the rest of the continent." She's also read most of the classics; she's actually read *War and Peace*, and *Anna Karenina*, and everything by Jane Austen.

Also, Mum can quote the Bible, chapter and verse, in a careless, offhand Anglican sort of way, although it was "those bitter, frustrated Catholic nuns in Eldoret" who beat it into her. And she knows the Latin for nearly everything. *"Adansonia digitata,"* she says. *"Acacia albida."* It seems likely they'd have understood her in Rome. She'd have fitted in too. "Oh, I've read heaps and heaps about the Roman Empire," Mum said. "Empires fascinate me."

Everything fascinates her.

She's transfixed by life.

There's too much of it, she's terrified of missing out.

To help assuage her terror, Mum always has three or four books on the go, plus whatever newspapers she's been able to get her hands on from Britain. Meantime, she also reads the *Times of Zambia* and the *Zambia Daily Mail* as well as the Lusaka *Lowdown*. It takes her forever to get through everything; she's a lifetime behind.

"I really need to be two people," she says. "I'll never catch up otherwise."

Mum reads every article in everything from start to finish. She scrutinizes each advertisement with detective-like attention or as if searching for hidden meaning, she avidly follows sports and the arts, and she absorbs every detail about the British royal family. She keeps a sharp eye on the financial markets, although they unnerve her. She leaves the obituaries for last, as a treat.

"I like to walk everywhere very slowly and look at things very carefully," Mum says. "Meanwhile, Dad charges off for the horizon like a madman. He loses the dogs half the time. The dogs prefer the way I walk; they like to stop and look at things too."

But she'd needed him.

She'd needed him for balance, even if it wasn't balance a casual observer would notice or appreciate as such. Dad hadn't pondered and wavered the way she did; he'd jettisoned and bounded. And he'd checked her impulses to root and stockpile. "It's been very trying for someone of my personality," Mum had complained. "I'm a hoarder trapped in a mad arrangement with a renouncing nomad." Mum gave a sigh of exasperated envy. "Rich built Van a whole separate thatched cottage just for her junk."

Nostalgie de la boue, the French say; nostalgia for mud, a longing to return to a kind of wanton ease, a murky complacency. Mum would have stayed there, but my father was like a bolting horse; a terror of sinking kept him plunging forward, not so much with a sense of direction as with a sense of urgency. He avoided mire, he shook off the excess, he honed, he scraped.

And after thirty-five years of this, Mum went on strike.

My parents had been between farms again; Dad had been between work permits again, between jobs. And Mum had had a complete nervous breakdown. After that, she'd lain in bed in a borrowed cottage on the outskirts of Lusaka with the dogs, and had refused to participate in any of Dad's harebrained schemes until further notice.

"I pulled a fetlock—strained brain more like—and had to go under the covers with the dogs," Mum said afterward. "I didn't have much choice, I was so exhausted. I think Dad was worried he'd broken me forever and for good. I think it gave him quite a fright when I stayed in bed a whole year."

But it worked.

Dad stopped scouring the Southern Hemisphere.

At the age of fifty-nine, Tim Fuller of No Fixed Abode finally resigned. He went on bended knee, hat in hand, to the headman of a remote and difficult district in the Zambezi Valley. He brought gifts—a shortwave radio, size 8 shoes—and he promised to bring jobs to the valley, and expertise. "My wife is a very good farmer," he'd said. "She's the expert."

After months and months of this, he had it in writing.

Henceforth he'd be Tim Fuller of No-Man's-Land.

My father delivered to my mother the title deed. He was granted two donkeys from the minister of agriculture to clear the land. When he'd cut a boundary, a triangle of a couple of hundred acres beginning in mopane woodland and ending at the Zambezi River, he drove Mum down to see their future farm. He'd put her in the shade on a camp chair with a thermos of tea and two boiled eggs. "Work out where we should put the house," he'd said.

It nourished them both, this eleventh-hour concession to take root somewhere at last, but only because it had been so hard won on both sides. She brought topsoil and plants from up-country; a jungle ensued, there was vibrancy. She got ducks and sheep. She got cats and puppies. Monkeys, birds, skinks, and frogs moved in, there were little animal faces behind every frond. Mum welcomes all but the most venomous of snakes, and even those she cherishes as much as possible.

"I ask them politely to leave the garden and the house. Very politely," she said. "But sometimes Dad has to shoot them. I don't like that; I feel rotten, such magnificent creatures, perfect skins. But what can you do? You can't have a black mamba sunbathing directly over the front door for months on end, can you? The staff was on the verge of mutiny." She paused. "And they do kill dogs. I explained myself to the mamba as clearly as I could."

Mum talks to animals incessantly.

I took notes once: By breakfast, Mum had already found and rescued a nest of baby mice, all the time reprimanding her erudite ginger cat Professor for his probable intent to murder the helpless, sweet little things. She'd held a delighted if respectfully distant conversation with a massive and beautiful cobra roped around the jesse bush on the path to the small dam. She'd spoken perfect paragraphs of poetry to a flock of white egrets leaving their roosts on the farm and going upriver for their morning commute.

"A pile of books on every piece of furniture," Dad complained happily. "And a dog on every pile of books." When they'd finally built a proper house, he'd made a corner for Mum in the bedroom where she could cordon herself off behind a desk, drape curtains from her mosquito-net frame around her bed, and luxuriate in her piles of books, her heaps of dogs, her pyramids of teacups.

Dad kept his section of the bedroom monkish neat. His drawers and trunk were organized like those of a soldier, everything folded precisely. Next to his bed, there was a rug on which Harry slept. Dad saved his excesses for public consumption.

IN HIS LATE THIRTIES, my father had been thrown out of a Greek restaurant in Rhodesia for breaking not only all the plates of the diners at his table, but also those of the diners around him. "Well, apparently," Dad explained afterward, his face set in blameless surprise, "we were at the *Bombay Duck* on Central Avenue. Not the *Aphrodite* in Strathaven."

By which mistake my father concluded that the touchiest Chinaman he ever met was the Rhodesian manager of Salisbury's most sincere attempt at Oriental cuisine. The Rhodesian manager was ex–British South Africa Police, a commander. It had given him the impression he could be anything, or anyone, he liked. "In those days, you'd never see an actual Chinaman north of the Limpopo," Dad said. "Now the whole of bloody Africa's Beijing South."

My father was British, he declared his Englishness until his death. Or he didn't pretend to be other than what he was, but he didn't defend the national character he'd been born to either. He'd been too stung by his own people, made too unwelcome by them, too early. Also, the country was small, belittling; it would have shrunk him to live there.

Anyway, over time, the English had eroded out of him; or he'd eroded the English out of himself until all that was left of his upbringing was a peculiar and dated brand of British insouciance. Or perhaps that's just what happens if you leave an illogical optimist of any nationality out in the full glare of life for long enough.

He'd become heroic, by which I mean, my father lived by his own rigorous if unorthodox rules. He had natural internal discipline, but he hated discipline imposed. And he never let anything get him down for very long, unless it was the sort of thing that is supposed to get you down; for example, a hangover, or a bad decision, or deadliest of all, a combination of the two.

Above all, my father was that ancient instruction fulfilled. *Nosce te ipsum*, know yourself. Know yourself to the core, and you will know everything there is worth knowing. Know yourself until there is nothing more to fear, or to hope. Know yourself, and since you'll know your place in the world, you'll *become* the world.

Then even if you lose your place in the world, you'll still be of it.

Even if your mind goes, you won't go with it.

And there is no distance for your soul to travel to find yourself.

DAD HADN'T JUST WOKEN UP THERE, liberated from the usual tethers of nationhood or identity. He hadn't just woken up, a white man in south-central Africa, dismantled to his essence, traveling light, moving fast. He'd gotten there the hard way; or he'd taken the hard way. Or he'd tried like most people to attach himself to an identity and the identity had insisted on blood in return.

He was English, and we were English along with him. Long after Mum and Dad had become permanent residents of Zambia they still received invitations to the Awful Dos at the British High Commission. The Queen's Birthday, all right-thinking Brits were supposed to celebrate that, of course, also royal weddings and coronations, if there'd ever be another one in our lifetimes.

But for six years, we'd revolted against Britain.

For six years, we'd been officially Rhodesian. For six years only, but it had made an indelible impression on us. It must have meant something to Dad too, because after he died, among his very few belongings I found a small, green leather-bound booklet given "to Timothy Donald Fuller with the Compliments of the Ministry of Internal Affairs as a memento on becoming a citizen of Rhodesia at Umtali on 17th October, 1974."

Inside the pamphlet were a few of the sorts of things meant to inspire Rhodesian citizens onward and upward to greater things. A statue of Cecil John Rhodes, looking gouty; that was page 1. Page 2 was a nearly illegible manuscript of a poem by Rudyard Kipling.

Following that was a list of My Duties as a Citizen of Rhodesia. These included nine instructions, the last of which was: "It is my duty to be just, tolerant and courteous to my fellow country-men...." I couldn't feel it then, at all. Our hypocrisy, the hypocrisy of white Rhodesians, was so official, so complete, so pathological we couldn't feel it ourselves. We could say one thing; we could believe and feel and do another.

THE NIGHT OF MY FATHER'S DEATH, I got back to my room late; it had been a long day, and I'd already spoken to Rich, broken the news. But I phoned Zambia again. Vanessa picked up on the first ring, already awake. Or she was still awake; she'd been awake for hours, she'd be awake all night.

"Oh, huzzit, man," Vanessa said now.

"Oh, huzzit, man," I said back.

We didn't speak to anyone else this way, in exaggerated accents, using slang from a country with no name, and as if we had no one to talk to but each other, as if the war were still on.

"Is she asleep?" Vanessa asked.

"I tucked her in myself."

"You what?"

"Well, I stood at the door and said, 'Good night.'"

"Oh," Vanessa said. "Slight exaggeration. You had me worried for a moment." I heard her light a cigarette and inhale. "Oh, this isn't going to be a picnic." She exhaled.

"We're supposed to have quit three days ago," I reminded her.

"I know," Vanessa said.

Then we listened to each other not speaking for a long time. It was a way to bridge the unthinkable gap between Kafue and Budapest, a way for Vanessa to burn the hours of talk time purchased for her phone from the kiosk by the railway line. Vanessa had stockpiled talk time when Dad was taken to the hospital, as if both talk and time could be bought, or brought back.

"I didn't say good-bye to him," Vanessa said at last.

"Me neither," I said.

I closed my eyes. I could picture Vanessa in her shawl, pacing the area around her veranda, her garden bathed in moonlight, the scent of lavender bushes and roses sweet and thick in the air. She'd have her phone to her left ear, her hair long down her shoulders, her right hand waving a silver-grey trail of cigarette smoke. Suddenly she gave a little gasp. "Oh, Al-Bo," she said. "Did you hear that?" She paused. "There it is again. Did you hear anything?"

"No," I said.

"The jackals are out tonight. It must be the moon; it's been such a big moon, hasn't it? It's got everything howling." There was a rustle while she held the phone away from her ear, but the jackals had stopped yipping by then, or they were too far away and faint for me to hear them.

"No," I said again.

"Oh, Al." Vanessa broke down. "Dad loved the jackals."

"I know," I said.

"Everything I ever did, everything I saw, or heard, it was to tell him about it," she said.

"I know," I said, but I didn't know, not really.

I couldn't know.

Each daughter experiences her father's death as if she were the only daughter on Earth, and he the only father. And to each daughter, a father is a particular set of facts, a peculiar series of circumstances. To think of him otherwise, to see him through another's eyes, feels like a betrayal.

He'd been one father to me, and another to her.

"I was always his favorite," Vanessa said.

"I know," I said.

WITH DAD AT THE HELM, our family of four had had mettle. We'd gone through hells of our own making, and hellish acts of God, and we'd always emerged from the flames, sooty, buckled, and staggering, a child down perhaps; but we'd emerged one way or the other, we bloody Fullers.

Until now, we'd always emerged, we four, we final, essential, skeletal family of four. Three seemed a vanishing number, the dead outliving the quick. There wasn't backup with three; no one to fall back on if a man went down. "Three bloody women in the house," Dad had always lamented. "No wonder I can never get anything done."

CHAPTER SEVEN

Make a Plan, and If That Doesn't Work, Make Another Plan

A t four-thirty a.m., a little more than a full day since Dad had died, I gave up my sleepless night. I made two cups of tea. I put sugar in both. Then I let myself out of my room, went down the hallway, and into Mum's room. I turned on the light and stood, fixed to the spot in disbelief; I'd have dropped the teacups, like they do in movies, except I'm fanatical about my morning tea. I put down both cups carefully, and then I panicked.

"Mum!" I said, addressing the heap of bedding.

I'm good and quick at assessing the scene of a crime, something I attribute to my inherited addiction to soothing murders with British protagonists and foreign detectives. "Twaddle or not," Agatha Christie's Hercule Poirot responds when he's falsely accused of reaching the wrong conclusion about the identity of Arlena Marshall's killer in Guy Hamilton's 1982 adaptation of *Evil Under the Sun*. "It's the only explanation which fits all the facts."

I adore Poirot's rigorous, logical little grey cells; I love the inevitability that the criminal perpetrators in his world will always be brought to justice. I'm comforted by Poirot's unassailable certainty that he's completed the investigation, and by sheer deductive brilliance he knows what he knows.

His truth is his line in the sand.

The whole thing's a balm to me.

"Mum!" I said again, shaking the heap of bedding.

It was clear that after I'd left Mum shortly before eleven the previous evening, she had decided to redo the packing entirely. Now, her once neat suitcase was bursting with plastic bags, sticks, and feathers. She'd semiwrapped the half-eaten block of crusty pink cheese in a hotel facecloth and popped that into an ashtray next to the little white vase with the fake daisy poking out of it.

Dad's duffel bag had been emptied too; most of his belongings were on the bed, in the bed, his clothes tangled up with the sheets. Also, there were now four empty wine bottles in the dustbin that hadn't been there the night before. Mum had draped Dad's socks over their mouths and necks, perhaps in the hope this made them look more like ornamental fake flowers, and less like four empty wine bottles.

"Mum!" I shook the heap of bedding again, more vigorously this time. At last there was a reply of sorts from beneath the layers of sheets, pillows, clothes, and comforters, a faint, slightly annoyed snore; the noise one of Mum's terriers makes if you try to boot it off a chair to sit there yourself.

"Mum!" I said again. "Are you awake? Say something!"

The top of Mum's head appeared. She looked a little like an annoyed terrier too, disheveled as a Jack Russell after a tussle with a monitor lizard. Mum's dogs will take on anything, mostly it's reptiles versus canines; it doesn't end well for the pets, usually. "Oh, hello, Bobo," Mum said.

"You're conscious," I said. "Thank God!"

"Of course I'm conscious," Mum said. She blinked at me blearily. "But I'm very sad."

"I can see that," I said.

"Terribly sad," Mum reiterated.

"Yes," I agreed.

Mum gave a hiccup. "We've got to get out of this place, Bobo."

"That's right," I said, encouraged. "Our taxi leaves in fifteen minutes. And look, I've brought you tea. I put in some sugar for the shock."

Mum disappeared back under the covers. "Okay," she said.

"So you should get up," I said, my voice rising.

Mum reemerged. "But I'm very sad," she argued. She sniffed. "You said it yourself, I'm in shock. I can't possibly get up."

I could see this was one of those customary circular conversations; they were a regular feature with me, Mum, and Vanessa; we'd perfected the art of the round. But instead of reacting as if this were normal for us, I reacted as if the hotel room were on fire; it was the fresh grief, I suppose. I lost my head completely.

"Mum," I shouted. "You have to get up. If you don't get up, we'll miss our plane. We'll be here for another week."

Mum reappeared, frowning. "Stop being so bossy," she complained. "And pessimistic. It's not helpful."

It wasn't helpful, I knew that, but I couldn't help myself; helplessly unhelpful. "Vanessa's the one you really want in a panic situation," Mum always says. "Nothing fazes her, really." Which is true until it isn't, but in any case, Vanessa would have coped much better than I in this moment. And if Vanessa wasn't coping, she knew instinctively how to get other people to cope on her behalf.

Dad coped too; it was one of his signature characteristics. I never saw him break down, ever. Or it took a spectacular accident, a coup, a national crisis to momentarily lay him down, but never down and out. "Make a plan," Dad always said. "And if that doesn't work, make another one and if that doesn't work, you're probably the problem."

I'd done it all wrong.

I'd gone without a plan, or a contingency plan. And in so doing, I'd unmade any plan I'd ever had. And I was now indubitably the problem. In the few minutes between getting out of bed and now, I'd managed somehow to lock myself not only out of Mum's room but also out of my own. I found myself alone in the corridor, keyless and without tea, in my pajamas, achieving all the conventions for the representation of Shakespearean female madness. I wasn't distraught, exactly, but I was distracted, my hair about my ears.

This wasn't how it was done, I knew that; I'd failed my first test.

Mum wasn't like other people; it seems an obvious thing to say, but she was supernaturally unlike other people, in very particular ways. For example, it wasn't always apparent if she was conscious or unconscious, even when you'd hope there was no doubt. Recently, she'd had emergency intestinal surgery in Lusaka— her third—during which the anesthesiologist had managed to paralyze her without knocking her out for the entire four-hour ordeal.

"He was Rwandan," Mum said. "And he was jabbering away in French to the Congolese surgeon the whole time. I told him I'd listened to as much of his boring conversation as I could and then I'd started to think about more interesting things, merci beaucoup."

The Rwandan anesthesiologist had denied Mum's account, but we believed her. Dad had taken away Mum's driving privileges years before. "She's incredible, your mother. She'll keep going long after grown men are felled," Dad had said with real admiration. "It takes a hell of a lot to knock her out, your mum."

I berated myself; I should never have left Mum alone the first night of her bereavement. I should have stayed with her. I could have stopped her repacking; I might have prevented her current condition. I pushed the button for the elevator, waited a couple of seconds, then flew down the stairs anyway.

OBVIOUSLY, I KNOW VERY LITTLE ABOUT HUNGARY. I was in the country for twelve days, and for that entire time, I went back and forth along the same few miles between the hotel in which we were staying and the hospital in which Dad was dying. However, I'll say this: If Hungarian hospital staff, taxi drivers, and hotel receptionists are an accurate indication of Hungarians in general, then Hungarians are my parents' kind of people; calmly upbeat in the face of disaster and tactfully practiced at removing the toppled bodies of foreign invaders.

"Daughter Fuller," the man at the front desk greeted me, politely unsurprised by my appearance as I came clattering down the stairs a few minutes before five, bedraggled and close to tears. The taxi driver had arrived already too; he was drinking coffee. He regarded me with concerned interest. "We are sorry, Daughter Fuller," he said.

"Thank you," I said. I frowned, did I know him?

"And now you go home," the receptionist said, as if that were a cure he knew something about, a cure he was offering.

"That's right," I said. I cleared my throat. "But I'm afraid I've locked myself out of both the bedrooms, and we're not quite ready." I paused. "And I'll need help with the luggage," I said. "I can't manage it at all."

"Okay," the receptionist agreed.

The taxi driver put down his coffee. "Don't worry," he said. "Like Bob Marley song. Everything is all right, Daughter Fuller."

I didn't want to disagree with the taxi driver, but it seemed easier he discover for himself how unlike the Bob Marley song things were in that moment for Daughter Fuller. I followed the men upstairs, the receptionist opened the door with his master key, and there was Mum, a listing, disheveled Jack Russell terrier, atop the bedclothes.

"Mum, you're up!"

"Yes."

"Madam Fuller," the taxi driver greeted her warmly.

"Mića!" Mum replied reaching out her arms. "Oh, I'm very, *very* sad! My husband is dead; he died, my love, he died."

"Yes, Madam Fuller," the taxi driver replied. He embraced her. She clung on. "I heard the news. You are sad. I am sad."

"You know each other?" I asked.

"Of course I know Mića," Mum said. She frowned at me over Mića's shoulder as if I'd forgotten the name of her favorite dog. "He's the hotel taxi driver." She sniffed bravely and patted Mića on the back. "Aren't you, Mića?" she said. And then, in more practical, clipped tones. "Thank God for you. My daughter's completely gone to pieces."

Mića, I won't forget his name; nor Ábel, the aptly named receptionist. "I'm going to be fine once this sadness wears off," Mum said as Mića helped her into her clothes. "Everything's going to be all right."

"Like Bob Marley song," Mića agreed.

"Exactly," Mum said.

Meantime, Ábel had somehow managed to close Mum's suitcase; it bulged, the seams groaning, but it contained everything now, including her pile of interesting things. He'd also produced a wheelchair, a bellboy, and two styrofoam cups with tea in them for the road. Between the two men and the bellboy, they heaved Mum into the chair.

"How do I look?" Mum asked.

I riffled around in her handbag for her perfume, the new fragrance by Yves Saint Laurent, Black Opium; an overwhelming stench. "Ah, my new pong," Mum said. "Dad bought it for me in the duty free at O. R. Tambo on the way here." I drenched her in it. I put on her dark glasses, a slash of iconic Dior red lipstick. "There," I said. "That's better."

"Everything is okay," Mića reassured us; he surveyed the scene like a satisfied artist, all the props in place, everything properly settled. "Don't worry. Everything is okay."

Which, of course, it was, from any distance at all; from any distance at all, we were okay. In fact, we were better than okay. We were two recently bereaved women going home to bury their dead. Our grief had been supported, believed, privileged. Our foreignness had been noted as a mitigating circumstance, a cause for further pity and not the reason for further horror.

"Of course it's okay," Mum said. She patted Mića's hand. "We know that, don't we?" She peered at me over her sunglasses. "It's going to be okay, Bobo. Don't worry. We'll make a plan. It'll all be all right. Won't it, Mića?"

MUM WAS MAGNIFICENT, there's no denying it; she kept up a conversation with Mića the whole way to the airport, all the while with her late husband of more than fifty years in an urn inside a cardboard box, clearly marked as such, on her lap. It would have been too much for most people, but not for Mum.

Admittedly, she slurred a little sometimes, landing hard on consonants then sliding off them unsteadily, but since both she and Mića were speaking in heavily accented broken English, it wouldn't have been easy for a casual bystander to tell that she'd been up all night, repacking.

Although the effort had clearly exhausted her; she fell asleep as soon as Mića and I wrestled her out of the taxi and back into the hotel wheelchair. I put the cardboard box on Mum's lap. She folded over it, like a protective slumbering cat. I wheeled her to the check-in counter; Mića went in search of food.

"She must use her legs to get on the plane," the check-in man said, looming above his counter to peer at Mum. "She must walk herself."

"She can't," I said.

"What's wrong with she?"

"Her," I said. "What is wrong with *her*?"

The check-in man gave me a withering look. "I'm not a doctor. You tell me what is wrong with she. I am asking the question. What is wrong with she?"

Mum was snoring a little. It was a deep sleep she'd fallen into, and sudden, the kind that catches long-haul travelers and children off guard. Her dark glasses were sliding down her nose.

"She's had a stroke," I said, as softly as I could.

"What is this?" The check-in man looked dubious. "Stroke?"

Mum stirred restlessly.

"A stroke," I repeated, louder. "An accident in her brain. She's had a stroke."

Mum jolted completely upright, suddenly wide-awake and in good voice. "I've had a what?" She sounded offended. "I've had a stroke? On top of everything else, I've had a stroke? Bobo, what are you jabbering on about? No, I haven't. I have not had a stroke."

"Yes, Mum," I said. "A stroke. You've had one." I made big eyes at her, so she'd know I didn't really mean it. Mum blinked at me in disbelief. I turned back to the check-in man. "How do you usually get people who can't walk onto planes?" I asked. "There are all sorts of reasons people need to be in a wheelchair. Why does it matter why she can't walk? She can't walk. Don't you have a ramp?"

The check-in man remained unmoved; the male equivalent of Jazmin, he even looked a little like her, I thought, preemptively resentful, unhelpfully touchy. "She must use her legs into the plane," he said again.

I took a deep breath. "Isn't Hungary in the EU?" I asked. I hoped to sound connected, authoritative.

"Oh, Bobo," Mum suddenly interjected loudly and clearly from behind me. "What rubbish." She glowered like an owl over her dark glasses, first at Jazmin's brother, then at me; her fingers gripped the cardboard box containing the urn.

"Mum," I said. "I can manage."

Mum gave me a withering look. "Push me up to the counter," she demanded. "Let me deal with this." I pushed her closer to Jazmin's brother. Mum took a moment to compose her expression; an air of wounded authority isn't easy to achieve while propped up in a hotel-issue wheelchair, but she managed it. "Listen, my man." Mum leveled her gaze intently. "I'm very sad. I am very, very sad and I must leave this place."

Jazmin's brother blinked impassively.

Mum took a breath. "My husband of fifty-one years died yesterday morning, here in Budapest," she said very slowly; her Memsahib Abroad accent, but with even heavier measure. "We came here two weeks ago to take the healing waters, but he died. Caput. Finito."

"Oh," the check-in man said, his expression changing.

"Yes, not very healing waters," Mum agreed. "We return to our homes like this: one in a box, one in a wheelchair." She allowed a moment of unlikely grace to settle on the scene. "But it's not your fault. It's not your fault at all. We just want to go home." She clutched the cardboard box more tightly. "We'd like to put this whole matter to rest. As quickly and quietly as possible."

All the rules always changed for Mum and Dad. I'd forgotten that; my parents moved through the world because of the resistance they met, not in spite of it. Some of this had to do with the side of history they'd landed on, and the side of history they'd backed. But some of this had to do with their basic natures; they were able to grasp on to hindrances and use them to pull themselves toward an acceptable solution.

"Oh," the check-in man said again.

Mića reappeared in that moment with Mum's snack. *"Köszönöm szépen,"* Mum said, reaching out her hands as if taking Communion from a priest. "You have been so kind, so kind. And this lovely gentleman"—she bestowed a smile on Jazmin's brother—"is going to work out how to get me onto the plane. Aren't you?"

Then she ate what Mića had given her, obediently and carefully. He watched her like a kindly, indulgent nurse. Mum watched Jazmin's brother like a hawk. Then suddenly, it was apparent we were moving. Mića was leaving.

"You are a good lady," Mića told Mum. "A brave lady." He refused my offer of payment. He told Jazmin's brother he'd be back another day for the wheelchair, as if we all belonged to the same small town, and had known one another awhile. He mopped his brow and bent to embrace Mum. They both cried a little; Jazmin's brother cried a little too.

I DON'T KNOW WHAT THEY USUALLY DO with people in wheel-chairs at Ferihegy Airport, but we were driven to the plane in an ambulance, four handsome medics in attendance like the 911 version of the Hungarian Chippendales, Mum regal as it was possible to be in the hotel's shabby black wheelchair; and from there she was foisted on board the plane with the trollies containing ham-and-cheese sandwiches.

She waved one last time at the city. "Good-bye, Budapest," she cried as the ambulance sped back toward the terminal. "Good-bye."

It was definitely like a movie, but much more surreal.

"I can't forget this city, I'll never forget this city." She smiled sadly at the airline stewards as they strapped her into her seat. "The last place we were together; my husband and I. Thank you. Thank you all so much. You've all been so kind." She pinned her nose to the window. "Oh, dear, how sad. Good-bye, good-bye."

I'd been unable to find two seats together; buying two air tickets from Budapest to anywhere at the last minute had been hard enough. I took my place near the back of the cabin; I put Dad under the seat in front of me. The whole plane reeked of Black Opium. The other passengers began to filter aboard, everything so stubbornly routine, as if death had not recently visited, nor displacement and despair. The safety talk was given in three languages, the plane took off; I stared out the window.

Central and then Western Europe lay beneath me, greener and hillier and emptier than I had imagined this late into a hot summer. Villages were swept into valleys along veins of glinting water; rivers and reservoirs, tiny mountain lakes; everything seeming ancient and long settled, the blood and sweat and mud of generations soaked into one place.

But armies had washed back and forth across these pleasant-looking little settlements too, and in living memory; these quietly innocent places, scouring bloody tides of armies, over and over again.

The bodies had piled up here too, everywhere.

The bodies were still piling up.

Done correctly, years of careful tending, it was still going to take more time to grieve the dead from all these tragedies than the living had left. And yet, those who forget to grieve, forget. Everyone knows the forgetful are doomed to repeat the past; the willfully forgetful too, churning up the past like bones in the field.

It still happens in Zimbabwe: A farmer tills up the war's bones.

There's no escaping this.

IN A DREAM I HAD a few weeks after Dad died, I was in an overcrowded taxi in India. Whatever city I was in, the place was thronging, the taxi was moving slowly; pedestrians, cattle, and vendors pressed against the window. Suddenly I caught sight of Dad in the crowd, pedaling a rickshaw. He was shirtless, pouring sweat, laughing. He pulled up next to the window of the taxi. I'd tried to find the taxi's door handle, a way to open the window; I was desperate to get out. "Dad!" I'd shouted through the back window, turning to face him as he receded and the taxi pulled forward.

"Dad!"

"It's okay, Bobo." Dad was still laughing. "It was just a life! It was just one little life." And then he was gone, absorbed back into the great throng of people from which he'd briefly emerged, and the dream over.

It was just one little life.

He'd wanted me to know that; or, the part of me that knew him best knew he'd want me to know that. It was sometimes hard in the mysterious, murky time of early grief to know where I thought he ended, and where I knew I began, but somehow, in a dream, we'd collectively come up with the idea that his life had been no more than what it was.

It was just a life; it was just a little life.

But what a riotous little life it had been.

PART TWO

A Widow's Farm

Chirundu, Zambia

The Day We Die

The day we die
the wind comes down
to take away
our footprints.

The wind makes dust
to cover up
the marks we left
while walking.

For otherwise
the thing would seem
as if we were
still living.

Therefore the wind
is he who comes
to blow away
our footprints.

—SONG OF THE SAN BUSHMEN,
FIRST NATION OF SOUTHERN AFRICA

CHAPTER ONE

If You're Going to Go to the Dogs, Go the Whole Way

Hello, Nikki."

I swiveled: the accent, the familiarity.

"Oh, hello, Harriet," Mum replied.

Most white settlers acquire a common look; weathered, but *weathered*. Too much, too fast, too young. I have the look myself, and I've lived only half my life under that southern sun; but it brands you. "Holiday?" Harriet asked.

"Yes," Mum said.

It usually takes a few attempts to get passengers from the terminal at O. R. Tambo International Airport in Johannesburg to the correct plane, and there are always howls of good-natured laughter as passengers disembark one plane—"What, nobody going to Kinshasa?"—then climb back onto the hot, airless bus only to be taken to yet another plane, also not going to Lusaka. Mum loved O. R. Tambo for this and other reasons. It reminded her of the good old days of travel, "a little chaos, old acquaintances renewed, and South African Airways are *very* generous with their tots."

Harriet indubitably belonged to Mum's show-jumping days.

She looked horsey, and as if she'd taken a spill or two. She was peering around now, though, searching; I knew she was looking for Dad, my parents traveled in a pair, like swans and fish eagles. There was nothing that could stop the next question from coming. I could feel it before she opened her mouth. She turned to Mum. "Where's Tim?"

Mum didn't skip a beat. "I'm afraid he's on Bobo's hip," she said. I lurched forward; the driver was doing circles at that moment. Mum pointed at me. "Do you remember my daughter Bobo? No, of course not. How could you? She wasn't middle-aged when you last saw her. And she's an *American* now." Harriet looked at me and frowned; I knew she didn't recognize me. Of course I'd changed in the three decades since I'd been sixteen. "It's her teeth more than anything," Mum confirmed. "They're very keen on their teeth in *America*."

Then Harriet's eyes slid to the box on my hip. It had been clearly marked on every side, and on the lid. HANDLE WITH CARE. HUMAN REMAINS. THIS WAY UP. I imagine it's fair to say that however shocking the change I'd undergone since Harriet had last seen me, it was nowhere near as shocking as the change Dad had undergone since she'd last seen him. She went ashen beneath her ineradicable sunburn.

"Oh, my God," she said. "Oh, Nicola, I am so sorry."

Mum nodded, and smiled bravely. "Thank you," she said. "It's been quite a performance getting him through the X-ray machines."

Harriet quickly brushed away her tears. "Oh, my God," she said again. "Yes, of course. What a bore."

"*Very* boring," Mum agreed; then she'd lifted her chin and offered us all a profile in courage.

Almost all the passengers on the bus, minus the obligatory

crying baby, had hushed to take in the show. I was half expecting an outburst of spontaneous applause, but at that moment the bus jerked to a halt once again, and we were ordered onto another plane, this time, the pilot assured us, almost unable to speak through his mirth, "to the correct destination, wherever that is."

Then the air attendant sashayed front and center; he was born to shine, he had magenta hair. He gave his name as "Kitty, short for Kenneth." He paused. "And I'll be your everything on our short but sweet flight up to Lusaka." He was fanning himself with the only safety instructions available to anyone on the plane. "Okay," he said. "Safety talk. Listen up. Here goes."

Mum loved Kitty at first sight.

"If we crash over water we're very lost," Kitty was saying. He also said, in the event of an emergency, "Take off your heels. Finish your drink. Then someone, for the love of Pete, save my hair."

Then Kitty catwalked down the aisle, spanking men who hadn't yet fastened their seat belts, swapping beauty tips with anyone whom he felt needed it, tending the wary. He stopped at our row, his eyes sliding straight to Mum. "Oh, honey," he said. "As soon as we're wheels up, I'm getting you a double."

"How terribly thoughtful of you, Kenneth," Mum said.

"Honey," Kitty said, blowing Mum a kiss, "you're *my* priority."

Then the pilot announced we all needed to switch off our cell phones, strap in, and prepare for taxi and takeoff, at which a pastor in the exit row leapt to his feet, brandishing a Bible, and prayed over us all fervently. Kitty leaned down and whispered something to Mum. She laughed; they clasped hands.

Mum *loved* the gays.

We knew one gay when we were growing up, if you don't count the lesbians, which no one did. Also, Robbie—not his real name, there was trouble enough for him as it was—wasn't known to be gay when we were growing up; he was the son of a poster-child Rhodesian. He had been expected to be a soldier, a rugby player, a hunter. Instead, Robbie went in for costume parties, mildly alcoholic divorcées, and my mother. He'd waited until he got to England for his obligatory gap year abroad to announce his passion for a London cabbie named Neville.

By then we were living in Zambia. My mother had recently inherited a tiny unexpected windfall from a Scottish aunt, and she'd been waiting for someone with whom to spend it frivolously. Robbie was manna from heaven. It was the first time in our experience anyone had ever *come out* as anything. On the whole, we'd rather have died—and killed—than have been who we really were. Mum had been thrilled to the hilt. "I've always been very fond of Robbie," she'd insisted. "What a brave boy." She was on the next plane from Zambia to London. She bought a dozen Ascot hats and two tickets to every show in the West End.

"Robbie," she'd announced, showing up on his doorstep looking fabulous, with duty-free champagne, cigars, and chocolates. This was back in the late 1980s. "I don't care if you do have AIDS. Put on an Ascot hat, and come with me to *The Rocky Horror Picture Show*!"

"But I don't have AIDS," Robbie had said.

"Oh," Mum had said, marching into his apartment. "I thought you all did." She'd paused in each room, as if inspecting billets, landing at last in the kitchen, which overlooked a tiny terrace garden. Then she'd shrieked her approval ecstatically: "What a sweet little flat. Where does Neville keep his teddy bears? We've all been hearing all about his teddy bear collection."

IT'S NOT A LONG FLIGHT from Johannesburg to Lusaka, three hours or so, a little more if there's weather. It can be bumpy; wind shears in the dry season, stormy in the rains. It's impressive, those thunderheads stacking up and up, towering like gigantic fists into the blazing clear-blue sky above. The pastor in the exit row was praying loudly and sweating on all our behalves. "So thoughtful of him," Mum said. "Meantime, we can keep enjoying ourselves." She waved Kitty down the aisle. "I couldn't have another one of those sweet little miniatures, could I, please, darling?" she said. "It's been a stressful couple of weeks."

"You're telling me," Kitty said, resting for a moment on the back of Mum's chair. "It's one bloody thing after the other, isn't it?" He slipped Mum a couple of little bottles, a can of mix, a fresh glass of ice.

"Kenneth," Mum said, glancing at me significantly. "You're very tactful."

Kitty smiled and swanned back up the aisle, riding the turbulence like a dancer. Mum took a sip of her drink, licked her lips, and looked out the window; it's a straight shot north from O. R. Tambo to Kenneth Kaunda International Airport. It's arid, the towns tiny and spread out, Zimbabwe blameless and placid at this distance. "From here," Mum said, "you'd never know the place was run by a bloody dictator, would you?" The plane gave a stomach-lurching plunge. The pastor upped his prayer volume. We laughed. "What fun," Mum said. "It's not bad, is it, Bobo?"

However, the closer our plane got to Lusaka the more Mum's attitude solidified from hilarious joie de vivre to dignified Dowager Duchess, a BBC widow, say, played by Dame Judi Dench or Helen Mirren. It was as if the initial joy of getting close to home was beginning to settle into something more serious for Mum. And after all the travel, the exhaustion was wearing in, the adrenaline wearing off.

"I'm returning to a widow's farm," Mum said, as the unmistakable *Brachystegia* forests of Zambia's up-country rushed to meet us. "I can't be seen to be soft, Bobo. People pounce on widows in this part of the world; I've seen it. They think you're feeble without a man. But they're not going to pounce on me. I'm going to mark my boundaries, and hold them." She sniffed. "Anyone who tries any funny business with me is going to rue the day. I'm a widow, but I am not a feeble widow."

She downed her drink then and waved her glass at Kitty. Kitty had given up with the miniatures somewhere over Botswana. He tore down the aisle now with a proper bottle, ignoring the pilot's warning we were in for a bumpy landing. He sloshed a final tot in Mum's cup. The pastor was praying in tongues. I held Dad on my lap. It was comforting in many ways to know that he wouldn't have said much more if he were alive than he did now he was dead.

He'd have been amused, but quietly so.

THE FARM'S DRIVER, Mr. Kalusha, met us at Kenneth Kaunda in Lusaka; he's a river man, born and raised on the banks of the Zambezi, and he stands out from urban or agricultural men as such. He has the triangular body of a paddler, and the squinting thousand-yard stare of a person who has lived both in bright sunshine and among crocodiles and hippos his whole life.

"Welcome home," Mr. Kalusha said.

I rushed past Customs and Immigration. "Oh, Mr. Kalusha," I said. I stretched out my arms for a hug.

Mr. Kalusha looked politely at his shoes.

"Oh, Bobo, do try to pull yourself together. You're making everyone very uncomfortable," Mum said; she didn't encourage fraternizing with the staff. She was unflinching.

"Our suitcases please, Kalusha," she said, intercepting any

further unsolicited theatrics on my behalf. "Can you manage, or do you need to get porters? It's already been a very tiring journey." She paused to glare at me. "And some of us seem rather overtired." Then she threw back her shoulders, and marched out of the airport into the perfect up-country Southern Hemisphere spring morning. "And the farm, Kalusha. It's waiting for me!"

"Yes, madam," Mr. Kalusha said, following her with our suitcases, trying to fend off both my offers of help, and the porters angling for a tip.

"Ah, thank goodness." Mum flung up her arms. "We're home, Bobo. You can smell it, can't you?" And I could. The dust, the woodsmoke, the manure, the garbage, the burning garbage, the diesel engines, the sunbaked grass; it was home. It would always be, I thought, my soul's geography, this place; his place.

It was my stop too.

These were my people, because in the end, they were his people. He'd belonged nowhere and to no one, but he was coming home to them, to an unmarked grave in the heart of the Zambezi Valley. Who'd have thought? The aunts would be churning in their graves.

"Just drop a match on me," Dad had said. "I should be pretty flammable by now." He hadn't been squeamish about the end; he hadn't been squeamish about much by the end, except the same things that had discomforted Mum and Mr. Kalusha, public displays of emotion, unless the protagonists were drunk, in which case public displays of emotion were not only tolerated but deemed a necessary nuisance. "The reason I have been known on rare occasion to behave badly when I'm drunk is to make up for being a bloody little angel when I'm not," Dad had explained.

WE DROPPED IN FOR TEA at the Rock on the way down to the valley from Lusaka; we always did. Roughly eleven dogs and about two dozen cats came out to greet us. One of Vanessa's elder children was at the Rock too; he had a young, pregnant wife and a small baby. Mum had been doing her best to rise above her part in it all; she'd drawn the line at becoming a *great*-grandmother. "I like children as far as they go," she'd said. "But they can go too far."

We settled ourselves on the veranda. "Just a quick cup of tea, and then we must get back down to the farm," Mum told Mr. Nixon. The closer we got to her beloved farm, the dogs, the more Mum sighed and looked at her watch. "Please tell the madam we are here, but hurry up, we won't be here for long."

There was a pause.

"If you could tell her to hurry." Mum sounded almost desperate.

Then my mother's great-granddaughter toddled up to her and put out a chubby little hand. After some hesitation, my mother grasped the child's hand and shook it politely but firmly; she detests a fishy handshake. "Pleased to meet you," she said loudly and slowly. "My name is Nicola Fuller of Central Africa." She'd met the child before, of course, but she took the precaution of reintroducing herself officially. "And what is your name?"

The child collapsed; any child would, and had to be rescued by its mother. "I'm sorry," Mum said, not sounding in the slightest bit contrite. "I thought it was showing off its manners. I didn't realize it wanted something from me. What does it want?"

Serenity, the child's name; it had seemed an optimistic and tranquil name to me. I'd liked it. Mum hadn't liked it much. I could tell, because she'd pursed her lips and groaned when she'd been told. And she'd pursed her lips and groaned even more when she'd been told there was another one on the way. "Oh, dear," she'd said.

"I am still getting used to being a grandmother; it came as a shock. Lots of little shocks, actually. It's not natural to me." Mum had shuddered. "Age, I mean. I'm not one of those people who is thrilled by it all. I'm not the knitting, scrapbooking type."

Serenity was mollified; scarred for life, but mollified. Then Mr. Nixon brought a tray of tea for us; he'd added a plate of Scottish shortbread imported from South Africa, as well as slices of fruitcake, Dad's favorite. "The madam is coming, madam," he reassured Mum. He'd thought of everything. We thanked him. He bowed and scraped backward off the veranda.

"Thank *you*," he insisted. "Thank you. Thank you."

Then Vanessa emerged onto the veranda from the bedroom wing, enveloped in shawls and scarves. "Oh, huzzit, everyone," she said, bestowing air kisses. There were effortless tears streaming down her cheeks; she swanned here, she wafted there, she settled like a large gorgeous butterfly in front of Mum. "I'll bet you're feeling a bit glum, Mum," she said. She paused. Mum stiffened, as if fearful Vanessa might be about to bestow a kiss. "I brought you something to cheer you up," Vanessa said.

"Oh?" Mum loves surprises, but only nice ones. She sounded suspicious. "Will I like this surprise?"

"Yes," Vanessa said. Then, like a Victorian medium, Vanessa's entire presence seemed to billow and swirl; with a flourish she presented from beneath her many scarves and shawls a small, squirming, perfect puppy. "Isn't she the loveliest color you've ever seen in your whole life?" Vanessa asked, holding the creature up for us to see. She *was* the loveliest color; blue-grey slate and shiny, like a sunlit grape, I'd have said, or like an ancient rubbed coin.

Vanessa plopped the puppy into Mum's lap. "She's going to be big when she grows up," Vanessa said. "Look at those paws. She's a mix of something and something else; I've got the papers. But don't worry. She had very proper parents," Vanessa explained. She took a breath and then added quickly, "American parents."

There was a momentary pause while Mum absorbed this unfavorable disclosure. "Not missionaries, I hope," she said at last. She'd had bad experiences with Baptist missionaries in the past, or maybe one of them was Seventh-day Adventist; they were *American* anyhow. "There's nothing worse than a Full Metal Jacket Bible Thumper. I've paid through the nose for their dogs before, and they've been duds."

It was strong language, for Mum to single out a dog as a dud.

But this puppy was wiggling on Mum's lap, and making hypnotizing yellow-green eyes at her, and Mum was having a hard time resisting her considerable charms. She picked her up; the creature deboned obligingly. "Well," Mum said, cocking her head this way and that, and staring deeply into the puppy's nascent soul. "You're very, very lovely whatever you are, such a lovely blue color." She kissed her new puppy on the nose; the puppy licked Mum's face. "Oh, yes, you are, and *very* intelligent. I can always tell."

Vanessa cleared her throat and said to Mum, "I thought of you right away when I saw the advertisement in the *Lowdown*. The Americans said they expect she'll make an excellent guard dog. She's had her shots, and whatnot. She's very official."

Mum beamed up at Vanessa.

Vanessa beamed back.

The puppy passed out from all the excitement.

"What will you call her?" Vanessa asked.

Mum tilted the shiny, limp little creature this way and that. "Oh, something *very* special," Mum said. "It will come to me. But it'll have to be something very special."

———

WE LEFT THE ROCK SOON AFTER TEA, the new blue puppy asleep on Mum's lap. Mum shut her eyes for most of the drive; I didn't blame her. Mr. Kalusha is an excellent driver, the best, but he isn't Dad, and it felt strange, out of place, disloyal even, to be driven home by someone else. Dad had flown down the curves on the escarpment past all the piled-up, gaping, broken-down lorries; then there was the first baobab, an indication we'd hit low elevation. "Tsetse flies, heat, and not so many people," Dad used to say.

He'd loved baobabs for that reason.

And after that, the little bridge with the crumpled guardrails a dozen miles west of the border between Zambia and Zimbabwe. The bridge was choked with goats, as usual. Mum opened her eyes then, all the bleating; Mr. Kalusha was leaning on the horn. "Oh," Mum said.

I didn't say it, I couldn't say it, but I thought it. "Nearly home."

I knew Mum was thinking it too.

It would be all right now if the little bridge collapsed, or if we hit a goat, or if the pickup suddenly had a cadenza and refused to budge another inch. We could walk from here. We were among our people, we were among *his* people; we were willfully understood, our passage was assured, our word was good.

We were safe, because he'd been celebrated here. "Fuller!" "Fuller!" "Fuller!" The shout followed the pickup; in a town with few cars a man is known by the vehicle he drives. Dad had become synonymous with this white Ford; it was new, only six months old, but he'd made such a fuss of showing it off. He'd always given lifts to people he knew, up and down that hot, sandy road. It had paid to know him.

"Fuller!" people shouted, and waved.

"Oh, Kalusha," Mum said. "They don't know he's gone, they think you're Mr. Fuller. They still think he's here. Oh, Kalusha, who will tell them?" And then for one split moment, her mask slipped. She'd looked at Mr. Kalusha with naked terror, her hands gripped around the comforting little shiny blue creature on her lap. "How will we manage, Kalusha? What will we do without him?"

THERE WERE THE DOGS.

Or there were more dogs.

"This family's going to the dogs," Dad used to say. "The whole way." Not just the four dogs they'd left on the farm when they'd gone to Budapest. Nor just the addition of the shiny blue puppy, but also one of the Jack Russell terriers had delivered five more on the spare bed in the guesthouse while Dad had been dying in the ICU in Budapest, a world away.

An unthinkable, unbelievable, unnatural world away.

"What a clever mother," Mum had observed, patting Coco on the head. "What lovely, fat puppies you've had." Mum decided to keep two of the males. "I need names," she said. She was usually very good with names: Che Guevara, Mapp, Smokey, Button, Brucie, Pippin, Bumi, Lucia, Coco, "Chanel, not nut," Mum always added.

"How about Buddha and Pest," I suggested.

Mum looked aghast. "Oh, that's not at all amusing, Bobo. That's far too close to the bone," she said; she sounded shocked at the suggestion. "No, no, no, Bobo. I'll have to come up with something else. And I need to come up with a very special name for my precious new blue baby." Mum smiled. "So that's something to look forward to, three new names for three new puppies."

It was comforting, the routine, the dogs, the life, the insistence on so much of it; it was easier not to feel such a terrible, echoing, repeated, drastic loss, the way I had in Budapest. The sterile cocoon of hotel rooms and airplanes and airports had lent grief the added dimension of isolation. The farm croaked and sang and yelped with life; it slithered and crackled and exploded.

Dad's death had felt so final in the hot streets of Budapest; now I wasn't so sure in the Zambezi Valley, still wild in ways, impassive but vibrant. The hippos shouting from the river, roosters calling from the village, wild birds and frogs. Nothing felt final; it was exactly as Dad had always said: "If I pop my clogs, you'll barely notice. Everything will carry on as usual. It will be all right."

And it was all right.

It wasn't perfect, and it wasn't what I wanted, but it was all right. And it was lively enough that I could believe it wasn't *the* end, just an ending. It was an inevitable ending, and heaps of inevitable beginnings—a new season, a new crop of bananas, new ponds of fish fingerlings, new piles of puppies.

Dad was gone; but life pressed in to fill the gap.

In fact, life pressed in so firmly, so exuberantly, like a jungle straining to cover every patch of bare earth, there was hardly room for the living. One had to assert oneself for space; Dad had always found that to be the case. "If I barked and wagged my tail," he used to say, "I'd get a lot more attention."

Coco and her litter stayed in the spare bed in the guest cottage; Mum stuffed towels in the cracks under the door. "Puppies are such snacks for pythons," she explained. The new blue puppy slept with Mum; there'd had to be a rearrangement of the pack, obviously, unavoidably hackles had gone up. Some of the Jack Russell terriers had had to be spoken to very firmly. But in the end, everyone settled down around the new Best Beloved; bruised egos, but nothing more.

I slept in Dad's bed; it was more than I could stand. A lifetime I'd burrowed into this smell; and now it would be fading, every minute, fading. I couldn't breathe him in fast enough. I burst into more tears.

"Oh, for goodness' sake," Mum had said. She can't abide sniveling. "There are hankies in the top drawer if you can wrestle it open." I couldn't manage the drawers. It made me cry harder, thinking of Dad flinging the furniture around in his nightmares. "It's all right, Bobo," Mum said. She was trying to be comforting. "I know it's sad. It's very sad. Very, very sad. But it doesn't help to go on and on about it."

Harry slept on the cotton rug next to me. Or rather, he didn't sleep. He kept getting up, and pacing from the library door to Mum's slightly air-conditioned, more opulent section of the bedroom, and back to his cotton rug. He'd been such a one-man dog, Harry. For him, Dad's absence, his failure to return, the fact of an impostor in his bed, it was all a horrible realization, an undeniable dawning of loss.

"I think Harry knows," I said.

"Of course Harry knows," Mum said from her side of the room. Her voice was slightly muffled by all the hangings and drapes she'd pinned up around her bed.

I stretched my hand out beneath the mosquito net and tried to pat his head. Harry whined, disconsolate. "Oh Harry," I said.

"Poor Harry," Mum said. "People who say dogs don't have feelings have no idea what they're talking about. Harry has enormous emotional capacity, don't you, Harry?"

"Yes," I said. "He does."

There was a pause. "I was talking to Harry," Mum said.

Harry gave another whimper.

"I know, Harry," Mum said. "Me too, old boy. Me too."

THE HOUSE ON THE FARM, Mum and Dad's final house together, was the only house my father ever designed and engineered from scratch; he also undertook to supervise its construction. "All the other wonky places we lived were not Dad's fault," Mum had said.

But this house was entirely Dad's fault.

It wasn't overly grand; ambition had not been its downfall. It consisted of a lozenge-shaped library, a hexagonal bedroom, and a rectangular bathroom with an attached donkey boiler outside for hot water, although the bedroom and bathroom doubled as libraries too; Mum keeps books everywhere. It's a very funny shape, obviously, the house; a whole bunch of walls at odds with one another.

As a result, it's falling down.

"Dad just made a few scratches with a stick on the ground one morning, and then he told some builder he'd fished out of the pub, 'Go ahead, build a house here,'" Mum had said. "The builder did his best, but it was a ridiculously difficult assignment. Also, he had to work with Dad's sun-dried bricks. They aren't very good. Half of them dissolved on the spot."

In addition to these handicaps, the builder apparently had pointed out that Dad had ordered the house be built on black cotton soil. Black cotton soil swells in the rains and shrinks into hard squares in the dry season. "Good God, what a fussy old lady you are," Dad had admonished the builder. "Just build the thing and we'll prop it up with a gum pole or two afterward if we have to."

So the builder did as he was told as best he could, and repaired to the pub for a long weekend afterward, to restore his mind. The foundation of the house buckled and cracked; ants build nests in the crevices. Also, the roof is tilting, and a few years ago the ceiling fan in the library spun out and nearly decapitated Vanessa's eldest daughter, Nastasya. On top of this, part of the library wall is falling down; you can see daylight. Snakes seep into the house that way.

There are bats everywhere. Harry has jumped through the windows—bursting through the shattering glass unscathed, like in the movies—and he's broken them all. Now, following Harry's lead, the entire pack of dogs rocket back and forth through the paneless holes, as they please, as do snakes sometimes, and more rarely but also alarmingly, I feel, rabid dogs.

"People have *entirely* the wrong idea about us," Mum had said. "Because of the books, I suppose." Mum owns them all: *Out of Africa*; *The Flame Trees of Thika*; *Northern Rhodesia to Zambia: Recollections of a DO/DC 1962–73*. She'd owned *My Life Was a Ranch* until *someone* took it and didn't bring it back.

"People think it's all pink gin and White Mischief all the time, but it's not. Mostly it's too hot for any sort of mischief, and there are snakes. You *need* the drink, for goodness' sake. And your father insists we live a very spartan existence. I blame that mediocre boarding school he went to: Latin masters, frequent canings, and boiled cabbage. The effects can be lasting, you know."

IT WAS TRUE; Dad had eschewed luxury.

It made a person soft; that had been his chief objection. Also, it inspired jealousy in others, then you ended up dying for whatever unnecessary thing it was, a maradadi watch, a fancy television, the latest cell phone. As to what constituted a luxury, Dad concluded that if most Zambians couldn't afford it, then it was a luxury.

Therefore everything was a luxury, including life itself.

"Your father is *so* absolutist," Mum had complained. "I think he gets it from the aunts." She had glanced reflexively at her shapely ankles. "They turned into do-gooders and Christian Scientists, you know; the ones that didn't drink. It's all about suffering in silence as far as I can tell, being a Christian Scientist, I mean. Drinking is about suffering sensibly. Anyway, you can't drink enough for this heat; you sweat the stuff out before it can do you any good."

The ordeal implicit in an ordinary Day in the Life of Nicola Fuller of Central Africa is something in which my mother delights. Or rather, she sometimes resents the ordeal, and she complained bitterly about my father's frugality, but she takes overt pleasure in her guests' shock at the picturesque but primitive chaos that greets them when they arrive at her home.

"They try to act cool as cucumbers, but it's not what they're expecting. White people living so simply, you can tell it shocks them. They say, 'Oh, your orange Le Creuset pots, how quaint. It's so open-air; look at your bird feeders. I simply adore your style, it's very authentic,' and they take lots of photos," Mum says. "But let me tell you, they drop their cameras in a hurry when the first reptile lunges out at them."

My father took quiet pleasure in shocking the guests too, he always did. "Excitement of the week," he'd write to me from the farm. "Guest attacked by python in the library," he'd once reported. There had been hysterics on behalf of the guest, understandably. "British charity worker," he'd added. I could tell this especially delighted Dad. He despised aid workers. He hated them, as far back as I can remember he's hated them.

"Bunch of bloody long-drop diggers," he'd mutter. He'd sometimes swerve pointedly into the road when he saw their SUVs. Save the Children, World Wildlife Fund, CARE, USAID, Oxfam. His eyes blazed. Mum clung on to the car door and pretended to protest; Vanessa and I said our final prayers.

"That'll teach the baskets to stay home and dig long drops in their own damn villages," Dad would say, eyes lifted to the rear-view mirror in unapologetic assessment, having driven the alarmed do-gooders into the bush. He'd brandish his fist out the window, a final defiant gesture. "Go home. Piss off. *Foutez le camp!*"

But Dad had mellowed with time.

Or he'd realized that if you allowed it, the world would do all the teaching that was required. Also, age had humbled him, exposed him. He reasoned he'd done at least as much wrong in his long, busy life as the do-gooders had in their short, lazy ones. So while I wouldn't say he went out of his way to invite aid workers to the farm, if they showed up, he was gracious enough. "You can have the guest cottage as long as you like," he offered. He didn't add that the guest cottage lacked hot water, fans, and a ceiling, and was preferred by the area's breeding frogs.

"I find luxury only encourages guests to outstay their welcome. A reptile or two keeps everyone on their toes," he'd said.

In recent memory, there'd been a German journalist reporting on postcolonial race relations in southern Africa; that visit had gone as expected. Then there was a suicidal Dutch microfinance expert; he'd redoubled his efforts at self-annihilation after a single night on the farm. And most notorious of all, there had been the Frog Croc Bird, a young French scientist who'd come to Zambia to study crocodiles; according to Mum she'd mostly poked around the poor creatures' reproductive organs.

"She was sponsored by some fancy university," Mum had said. She'd paused, and then added, "A well-endowed institution, I'm given to believe. Although their budget didn't seem to extend to laboratory coats." Mum shut her eyes against the memory of the vision. "The Frog Croc Bird's outfits were like the American cocktail hour—jarringly brief. It nearly bankrupted us. I couldn't get any of the men to do a stroke of work for me on the farm for months."

"What did she find out about crocs?" I'd asked. "Anything interesting?"

But Mum didn't know; the Frog Croc Bird kept her findings to herself, or to the paper she'd published in France long after the memory of her too-brief outfits and her molestation of the local wildlife had faded in the malarial haze of another rainy season. "She didn't send us her article, so I know nothing of her conclusions," Mum had said. "Nor did she ask us any questions, which I thought was odd. Crocodiles are the natural enemy of the fish farmer, Bobo. That Frog Croc Bird could have learned an awful lot from me if she'd bothered to ask. I know my enemies well, very well." She paused thoughtfully. "It's the Highland blood, I suppose. The very distilled blood, to be precise, of the Inner Hebrides archipelago."

STEEP STAIRS PLUMMET through Mum's jungle of a garden to the kitchen. Cobras, black mambas, and pythons prefer her garden to any other place in the Zambezi Valley; also there are several monitor lizards and a half dozen crocodiles that live between her garden, the fishponds, and the irrigation canal. The dining room and sitting room aren't rooms, there are no walls, just a roof propped up by a few dissolving brick pillars; animals and humans come and go as they please, vervet monkeys spill around, stealing sugar and bananas off the dining room table.

"It's a death trap down there," Vanessa had said. She had refused to visit ever since her sixth child was born. "Dad won't put a fan in the guesthouse, or netting. You lie there in a puddle of sweat getting dive-bombed by bats the whole time. Dad says they're a tremendous luxury; live mosquito control."

Mum eschewed luxury too, not because she didn't long for it—she craved it wholeheartedly—but because it terrified her. She was scared of breaking things, she had a tendency to pull knobs off machines and to microwave tinfoil. The sight of white carpets and pale furniture made her spill tea and red wine compulsively. Automatic paper towels in public restrooms made her scream and leap into the air. "In my experience something shooting out the wall is not usually benign, let alone hygienic," she'd explained.

Air-conditioning in America made her sick, it was always turned down so wastefully low; so did the air-conditioning at the Rock. Still, she pined for moderate coolness. "Just a tiny puff of relief from the unrelenting swelter," she'd said. She wanted her own little patch of pretend-Simla-away-from-Calcutta, her imaginary bungalow in the hills, an invisible swath of up-country. "It's like absolute dog years to make it through a single rainy season in the Zambezi Valley," she'd complained. "The heat. The humidity. I feel a hundred by four o'clock every afternoon."

Dad hadn't appeared to believe Mum's complaints of nausea and dizziness were caused by heat, or that it was possible even to be sickened by heat, but when both she and one of the larger dogs, Smokey, had nearly died of heatstroke on the same afternoon, both of them spiking fevers in the odd-shaped sweatbox of a hexagonal bedroom, Dad had finally agreed to the addition of a single air-conditioning unit.

"You really do have to be without a pulse for the better part of an afternoon before Dad will take you seriously," Mum had reported with understandable outrage. "For weeks and weeks it's been about forty degrees centigrade, and a million percent humidity. That's seriously hot. The bananas were flopping over. Poor Smokey nearly croaked. I nearly croaked."

Dad had instructed the farm electrician to put the unit over Mum's bed, behind all her drapery that hid from his view her dogs and books and teacups and special collections. The effects of the air-conditioning barely wheezed over to his side of the room, kitty-corner/dogleg across from hers.

He was a creature of habit, discipline, and in spite all his frenetic whirring about, he was also a creature of routine. He slept in his wedge-shaped corner of the bedroom on a simple wooden bed, with a thin blanket from the Chirundu market. Since he was habitually intent on rising before dawn, there weren't curtains on his side of the room, and as in the rest of the house, nor were there windowpanes. At night, Harry flopped down on the cotton rug by Dad's bedside and slept deeply.

They both had been in the habit of retiring early, rising before the sun.

"Old dogs aren't gorgeous by accident," Dad had said. "Good night, everyone, see you all at sparrow's fart."

He had slept beneath a mosquito net, face to the door, back to the wall. He had never set an alarm, but in the pinking half hour before sunrise the mosquito net around Dad's humble little farm-made bed had parted. His bandy legs had swung out; then there he was shaking out his slippers, spiders mostly, or rose beetles if there'd been a recent hatch of those. "Good morning, Harry." Dad had always addressed Harry with the utmost cordiality. "Did you sleep well?"

After that had come the routine of deflecting the flock of Jack Russell terriers swooping off Mum's bed, a morning exercise regime, a lot of bending, and kicking. "Go on, get out of here, you horrible little rats." Dad had stopped bothering to learn the terriers' individual names after the so-called Bloody Sunday massacre.

"Bloody Sunday." Mum's green eyes instantly rim red at the memory. She'd been taking her usual afternoon walk, a Sunday-afternoon walk, obviously. There was a sudden noise in the banana plantation; all the dogs went crazy. But before she had time to wade in and bludgeon it to death with her walking stick, a massive Mozambique spitting cobra had killed four dogs on the spot; another dog managed to stagger back to the yard before dying; and two had died in the night.

"The venom of these cobras replenishes," Mum had explained. "So it could just keep killing and killing until I managed to get a good whack at it. It was a day of such dark devastation. I'll never be the same. I'll never get over it."

The part I couldn't get over was the vision of Mum wading into the confusion of a dozen frantic dogs and one large, terrified, wounded cobra and then killing the reptile with one of her walking sticks. She loves her walking sticks; they're handmade by a blind man at the Chirundu turnoff. She'd broken it in the battle. "Precious," she'd agreed. "But not as precious as the fallen faithful."

She'd replaced the fallen faithful with a dozen new puppies, and as some of those had also met an untimely demise, she'd acquired a couple more, or a half dozen; she'd bred a few of her own litters. It became hard to keep track of the fallen Jack Russell terriers, let alone the flocks and flocks of new ones; Dad regarded most of the dogs under knee height as interchangeable.

"Go on, get by, you bloody little terrorists. Harry, bite them!" But Harry was a lover, not a fighter. In spite of his large size, his swaggering attitude, Harry was a lover of everyone except people on bicycles. He hated people on bicycles. He'd put on an uncharacteristic turn of speed and chase down a bike with the agility of a scrappy jackal. Once Harry had even managed to sink his teeth into a Danish aid worker on a motorbike; Dad had blushed with pride.

Harry was born to accompany Dad.

"Right, Harry, farms don't cock themselves up without assistance," Dad would say, opening the door from the bedroom to the library. Jack Russell terriers rained down and around Harry and him like confetti. I loved those mornings, staying on the farm in a spare bed in the library. Dad's morning routine was like a comforting radio drama to which I awakened with delight.

"Top of the morning, Bobo. No pythons in the night?"

"Hi, Dad. Nope, still here," I'd say.

"Well done. Well done," and then he'd be gone, with Harry by his side, a dog of great spiritual intelligence, it was easy to see, a dog of dignity and grace, a dog who'd learned to let fools be fools on their own time, with one notable, exceptional prejudice— anyone on two wheels.

He hated anyone on two wheels.

"Yes, well, I understand that," Mum had said. "I too never forget mine enemies." She sniffed; it was the sniff she used before throwing down her gauntlet. She'd won the Scripture Knowledge prize three years in a row at the convent in Eldoret under the tutelage of those sour nuns. "They put a lot of emphasis on the Old Testament at that place; it influenced me greatly." She paused to glare at me, as if any slip from the influence of God's ancient instruction had been my doing. "But I do find Second Samuel twenty-two, verse thirty-eight, pretty unequivocal, Bobo. The Bible is very clear; people are forever smiting their enemies."

I AWOKE BEFORE MUM that first morning on the farm without Dad. It was just beginning to get light, the sky streaked grey and pink. It was my favorite time of year on the farm; a good month, the Southern Hemisphere spring equinox. The days were hot, the nights nearly perfect; the dry-season wind had died down, but it was not yet dripping humidity.

Also, life was returning to the place. The mopane leaves were beginning to sprout, tiny spears of hopeful, vivid lime green against all the parched dry-season grass. The baobab trees too, those were beginning to bud. Birds were nesting in the swamp between the house and the bananas. Snakes, energized by the heat, were more visible and active; there'd be pythons in the sheephouses before long.

I parted the mosquito net and swung my legs out. "Hello, Harry," I said quietly. "Did you sleep at all?" Harry gave me a mournful look, and sighed. He had his head in his paws; he didn't bother to lift it. "I'm sorry," I said. I patted him. "I miss him too." Harry raised his eyebrows at me, penetratingly.

"Bobo." Mum's voice emerged from behind her self-made boudoir. I think it's not an accident she keeps a copy of Robert K. Massie's 1967 *Nicholas and Alexandra*, liberally doused in Blue Death, on the bookshelf closest to her bed.

Aside from being German and her silliness with Rasputin, Tsarina Alexandra had a very elaborate mauve boudoir in which she spent much of her time in splendid repose on a chaise longue; Massie makes much of this. There are photographs of this boudoir in the book; there's a suffocating emphasis on drapery. There are piles of books and papers on a table within reach; it's clear Alexandra was a collector of interesting things, a hoarder, a magpie-minded person, saved from the worst symptoms of *nostalgie de la boue* only by her many servants.

Sometimes you can tell where Mum gets her ideas, usually good ideas, inspired ideas, she'd have said.

"I think Harry blames me for Dad's death," I said.

"What rubbish you do talk, Bobo," Mum said; the drapes and cloth hangings around the frame of her mosquito net shook. Her hands emerged, clutching the shiny blue puppy. "Harry is heartbroken, just like I am. And since you're up, I'm gasping for a cup of tea. Also, here." She thrust the puppy at me. "Duna can't keep her little legs crossed another minute."

"Duna?" I said. I took the puppy. She wiggled and squirmed and squeaked; she peed on me.

"Clever Duna," Mum said. "Did you see that? She waited until she was off the bed before she uncrossed her legs. She's a very intelligent creature. I knew it. I knew it right away."

"Duna?" I said again.

Mum disappeared back into her self-made boudoir. A veil, or rather a sarong she'd picked up on a working holiday in Thailand, came between us. "It's a perfect name for her, don't you think?"

I looked into Duna's eyes. They were not unlike my mother's; pale yellow-green, very alluring, enchanting.

"My Blue *Duna*," Mum said.

CHAPTER TWO

In Times of Excessive Difficulty,
Cope Excessively

All the regulars at the pub at the bottom of the farm—this included some of the higher-ranking officers of the Zambia Defence Force, a couple of Customs and Immigration officials, and a few dipsomaniac fishermen from Lusaka—knew Dad's banking business. They were invited to sit with him, console and advise him, while he conducted it. "Better make it a double, Shupi," Dad would say. "It's my day for online fucking banking, excuse my French."

Shupi made it a double. Hippos submerged off the tip of the island opposite the pub shouted their condolences. Harry put the pub's resident Jack Russell terriers in their places, then flopped down next to Dad's barstool with a sigh. There'd be no dancing in the banana plantation today; Harry could feel the online-banking blues in his bones. He stared despondently across the river at Zimbabwe; even they, a failed state without a currency to call their own, couldn't escape it.

"Your good health, Shupi," Dad always said, opening his computer's lid. "Mine's about to take a turn for the bloody worse."

Then there'd be a delay, punctuated by a lot more cursing, while Dad went through the whole rocket-launch procedure of turning on the dust-menaced laptop, waiting for the pages to load, laboriously entering his passwords. He was always being bounced back to screens asking for more details.

"Why do they want to know my mother's maiden name?" Dad had asked. "She didn't know it herself half the time."

"It's a security question," Boss Shupi explained.

"Where was I New Year's Eve 2000?" Dad was incredulous. "How the hell am I supposed to remember?"

"You were here, Mr. Fuller."

"I'll put, 'In bed by nine.' Maybe they'll increase my overdraft."

My father's computer was an elderly, pampered Sony he'd bought at the duty free in O. R. Tambo back when the airport was still named for Jan Smuts, the prominent South African pro-British imperialist and son of well-to-do Afrikaner farmers. Jan Smuts had a whole string of letters after his name by the end of his life. Field Marshal the Right Honorable Jan Christian Smuts, PC, OM, CH, DTD, ED, KC, FRC.

It's clear that whoever was coming up with the honorable acronyms didn't see into this dishonorable future. "We're orphans of a defunct empire," Mum had declared. "Very few people understand what that really means anymore." She had taken a deep breath. "One has to be very humble, very grateful. You can't live in a country like Zambia if you aren't."

Meantime, O. R. Tambo, along with all other black South Africans born between the mid-seventeenth century and 1994, hadn't been given a chance to amass a string of letters after his name. In fact, Oliver Reginald Tambo had been deemed only fractionally human at his birth in eastern Pondoland in 1917; humanish, but not entitled to ordinary human rights, and subject to a boundless number of human wrongs.

He'd wanted to be a church minister, Oliver Tambo had. He'd wanted to be a quiet, bookish, peaceful man of God. He'd fished insects out of the bath, he hated killing so much. But in the end, Oliver Tambo had seen no alternative but to turn away from the pulpit and toward the paramilitary wing of the African National Congress. "Yes," Mum had agreed. "I love the airport, but I don't love South Africa. The Afrikaners took it too far, the blacks are bolshie, and you can't blame them; I find it very creepy, all of it. Just look at that Oscar Pistorius."

MY FATHER WOULDN'T HAVE KNOWN who Oscar Pistorius was. He died without knowing a single thing about the Kardashians. He'd stopped being up-to-date with British politics after the Falklands. But he wasn't removed from life, he was removed from the stories that swirl around the legs of a life, tripping it up. For example, although he knew very little about American history, or pop culture, he'd fundamentally understood the place, cut to its original wound. "A bit racialist, aren't they?" he'd observed.

He didn't acquire information, he didn't see the point of stockpiling facts; the whole enterprise of a twenty-four-hour news cycle seemed to him both pointless and tragically self-fulfilling. Helped by deafness brought on by the war, he'd honed his mind to neutral. "I didn't realize what an effort it is to stay ignorant," he'd said, leaning back and lighting his pipe. "You can't look anywhere without accidentally seeing the news."

Still, the ancient television was unveiled from beneath its protective dog-hair-covered blanket for the Nightly Bloody Whine, as Dad called Sky News, also for Formula One racing and Mum's cooking shows. The rest of the time, it sat like a monstrous, ancient pet in the corner of the library. Wasps had nested in the works, so it no longer played Mum's collection of beloved videocassettes, "but the sound still works," Dad had said.

In keeping with this rationale—that a horse, vehicle, or machine properly bedded down for the night lasted longer than one that wasn't—Dad had stored the one and only laptop computer he'd ever owned in its original packaging, except on his days for online fucking banking; then he'd eased it out of its cardboard box, raised it from its Styrofoam sarcophagus, and cradled it down to the pub on his lap, driving over the bumps and potholes with extra caution. In spite of this, Dad's computer had often stalled, and it had crashed frequently. Finally, it had died, refusing to produce even the tiniest pulse of light, no matter how many buttons Dad pushed. "It's passed out again," Dad had said, showing Boss Shupi a blank screen.

"It's an old computer," Boss Shupi had pointed out.

"Rubbish," Dad had said. "I've had it only twelve years."

He owned socks that were older, he'd argued. He had hankies and underwear that had outlived this machine. He'd even managed to keep a pair of leopard-skin slippers since 1963; and that was through hell, high water, and several hostile southern African border crossings. "Plus Mrs. Fuller's dogs," Dad had said. "And I haven't let a dog near this bloody thing. It's lived in its box since it was born. What's its problem?"

It was Boss Shupi's unhappy lot to explain to my father the principle of built-in obsolescence. My father had been shocked. "He's very naïve, poor Dad," Mum had explained afterward. "We both are. Very innocent and gullible." My father had mentally dropped anchor somewhere in the early 1950s; he'd stopped trying to keep up with mod cons after the invention of the microwave.

The startling news that even in his seventies, well beyond what he'd considered his natural shelf life, he was likely to outlive his computer had appalled him; he'd been indignant, furious.

"That's just bloody daylight robbery," my father had protested. "Do you mean to say that if I want to do my online fucking banking, excuse my French, I have to buy a whole new computer every twelve years? Who lets these bloody bastards get away with this?" My father had glowered. "I'd better have another double on the strength of that, Shupi," Dad had said. "Humanity's reached a whole new low."

My father had been constitutionally predisposed to hate the world of passwords and security codes and computers anyway. There was nothing life enhancing about any of it, he felt. But the dishonesty of deliberately manufacturing and selling something that was designed to blow up was not only criminal, in my father's view, but also obviously shameful. "How does that man manage to keep a straight face?" he'd asked. "He's laughing all the way to the bank."

In the end, Dad's unresponsive Sony laptop had been resurrected, with some glitches, by a Tonga computer technician/hacker who kept hours in a dusty kiosk in the Chirundu market. "I left it with Comrade Malambo for the morning, and by the afternoon he had it humming along like a bee," Dad had said victoriously. My father had considered his revived computer a triumph of Zambian ingenuity over Western corruption.

"I should write a letter to that bloody crook," Dad had said.

"Which bloody crook?" I'd asked.

"The smarmy one," Dad had said.

Dad had considered all computer manufacturers smarmy, but he'd focused the balance of his ire on the most visible and vocal offender, Bill Gates. He scoffed at the Gates Foundation's pledge to eradicate malaria, TB, and AIDS in sub-Saharan Africa, presenting as evidence for Bill Gates's uselessness the recently defunct Sony laptop. "Why would anyone trust that crooked bastard near a cure for malaria?" Dad had asked. "He can't even do his own job with a straight face, and he's trying to be a bloody doctor now. Well, between giving him the job, or Comrade Malambo, I'd put my money on Comrade Malambo any day."

Then rumors circulated, confirmed as always by the BBC World Service: The Gates Foundation had donated $50 million toward a mass-circumcision campaign in Zambia and, of all places, Swaziland. "What did we ever do to Bill Gates?" Dad had asked, crossing his legs and covering his lap with his red-spotted hanky; he could sound hysterically distraught when he chose. "I'm putting in an order for a chain-link codpiece for both Harry and myself," Dad had said, his voice going up two octaves. "Any other takers? Shupi?"

"Circumcision, Hon," Mum had clarified. "It's not the same as castration."

"Oh, dear God!" Dad had shrieked. "The family jewels. Run for the gomos, Shupi! They're coming for the family jewels."

My father had believed people who made a killing for a living shouldn't be let out among the general population without proper adult supervision, also not without a leash and a cattle prod. People who didn't touch soil, and who didn't have to rely on the genuine forbearance of their fellow humans, got unnaturally puffed up in his view, dangerously so. It didn't do anyone any good, even the puffed-up people. Manufacturing an endless supply of self-imploding computers, and getting away with it, deferred necessary humility; it encouraged a person to take the same flight path as Icarus.

"And it's only a matter of time before some touchy bastard

pushes the wrong tit on one of these things and blows the world to smithereens," Dad had said, paraphrasing cybersecurity concerns the world over. "And for once nobody will be able to blame me. I can't even turn my bloody computer on half the time."

Dad preferred a premechanized world, or a world humbled by vagaries. Without machines, or with more rudimentary machines, it wasn't so easy to steal from the past, or to promise a future in which you ignored the present. In a world before drilling equipment and center pivots and online anything, you were at the mercy of the very stark here and now; your beliefs tested, your integrity tried in real time. There was nothing virtual about it.

"It stops you getting too big for your boots," Dad had argued.

By which he meant, without the aid of technology, you did your seedbeds, you plowed your fields, then you lifted your eyes skyward, and you prayed. You went to your knees; in a bad year when the rain didn't come until December, you wore your knees to nubs. It shaves something off a man to be that vulnerable, subject to the sun and to offshore currents two countries away. It shaves something off a man to know there are impassive, massive limits to what he can do and no limits to what can be done to him. "You don't get anything from suffering itself," Dad had told me. "Except suffering, and more suffering. The trick is to suffer spectacularly, and then you still have suffering, but at least it's on your own terms."

DAD DIDN'T CELEBRATE BIRTHDAYS, he didn't see the point; it wasn't a trick to be born. But not everyone could face misfortune with the requisite stoicism and illogical hilarity. Not everyone could risk everything season after season, and then celebrate disappointment as if he'd won the lottery, or as if he were attempting to live Rudyard Kipling's British-boarding-school-permeating poem "If—" to the letter. "Triumph and disaster, Bobo," Dad had said. "They're the same coin, different sides; it's worth remembering."

It had happened over and over. There'd been eelworms in the bananas, so he and Mum had torn up the crop, made of it a maze at the dead ends of which were bottles of booze, and invited everyone in the valley to go wild for two days; that had been in our farming-in-a-war-zone era. Or there'd have been a drought, the maize stalling at shoulder height, tasseling under baking, cloudless skies; then we'd be in for a monumental rain dance. "Before the bank manager notices," Dad would say; these calamities were celebrated until at least one person, usually my father, was in drag. But after that, we'd be under the auspices of one of Dad's not-infrequent austerity plans.

"Everyone take in your belt a notch," he'd give the order.

Mum groaned. She hated Dad's austerity plans. They made her long for luxuries she'd otherwise been quite content to do without. Suddenly she craved caviar and champagne. She longed for escargot swimming in butter and garlic. "Such a succulent dish; so French, it even comes with its own little ashtrays." Also, the idea of never again going to the West End in a fabulous hat—designed to annoy theater lovers everywhere, you'd need a periscope to see around Mum—or the Bolshoi Ballet, that tore into her. "Never, ever, forever," she'd bemoaned.

"Nothing's forever," Dad would remind her.

Mum had a special look she gave Dad when he dared get philosophical on her. "Oh," she'd say, rolling her eyes. "How inspiring. Deep Croak. You should write a book of Dad's pithy and comforting sayings, Bobo. Maybe I will." But Dad was always right; a season or two would pass, some seasons would pass. And once in a while everything hit just right; the rain, the sun, the markets. Then they'd be flush with money, and we could let out our belts again. There might even be a trip to Paris, or in the end, the poor man's Paris.

The Paris of Africa was out of the question. Luanda, Angola, was routinely voted the city with the wealth, the fancy restaurants, the centuries' old European architecture to carry off the nickname; it was a single border crossing from Zambia, but only the filthy rich and the dirt poor could afford that place. There had been war there longer than anyone could remember, generations of war. All that oil, those diamonds, the ivory; it was too much.

"According to Paul Theroux, the whole country is now smothered with dictators and half-dead peasants," Mum had said. "You haven't read *The Last Train to Zona Verde*, have you, Bobo? I have. I'm Theroux's biggest fan. The poor man hated every moment; and he's been to Turkmenistan and places like that, so he'd know." As a result, Angola was not on a list of places Mum wanted to visit. "But I find it very interesting when other people subject themselves to hell on my behalf," she'd said. "It's very refreshing."

Mum was more accustomed to being subjected to hell on her own behalf. When Dad had finally been able to coax Mum down here to their final farm in the Zambezi Valley, to the scrubby patch of no-man's-land between the border post and the Kafue confluence, they'd slept on camping mattresses on the ground under mosquito nets tied to a mopane tree for a season, and then in a hut made of reed mats for a few more.

"No, Bobo, even for me, it was quite primitive and difficult," Mum had said afterward. "I don't think anyone can appreciate quite how primitive and difficult." I had tried to appreciate quite how primitive and difficult, and it had frightened me, honestly. My parents, heading for the age at which most people are considering retirement, had taken it upon themselves to start over, yet again, on a young couple's place, not a place for people soon to be the world's most reluctant, slightly appalled great-grandparents.

"Mm," Dad had agreed, puffing on his pipe. "I did it for Mum more than anything. She gets bored if things are too easy."

The mosquitoes in the valley are like jackals, the heat's abusive, the soil is shallow, and the river rises and falls at the capricious whim of the Zambezi River Authority, a joint effort between Zimbabwe and Zambia, and overseen by the Chinese, to manage the hydroelectric station upstream. "We all expect to get swept into the Mozambique Channel in a huge tsunami when the dam wall fails any moment now," Mum had said. "Three and a half million sub-Saharan Africans will drown, the BBC even had a whole special report on it, can you imagine? Three and a half million, and then you start to matter to the Brits. They'd care if they knew my Jack Russells were in peril."

AFTER MY FATHER DIED, I was surprised by some of what he'd kept over the years; baffled by what it meant about him, or what he'd thought it had meant about him. In the top drawer next to his bed, where I found the green leather booklet commemorating his brief conversion to a Rhodesian citizen, I'd found a few other markers of his life, such as they were; proof that he'd stamped the world with his violence, his seed, his passion, his sorrows.

There was, for example, a thin exercise book—the paper was rough newsprint, left over from Zambia's socialist days—in which Dad had recorded every drop of rain that had fallen near or around him going back thirty years. There were the birth certificates of his five children, and the death certificates of three of them. He'd also kept the telegrams read out at my parents' wedding reception. One of them made no sense, at least not in the context of marriage.

"ALL THE VERY BEST TO YOU (STOP) DON'T HANG AROUND THE BASE OF THE SCRUM, TIM (STOP) GET IN AND PUSH (STOP) THE FORTHERGILLS." I read it aloud to Mum. "It sounds suggestive, in a very 1964 sort of way," I observed.

"Does it?" Mum didn't agree. "I think it sounds very outdoorsy and wholesome. It's a rugby reference, Bobo. Let me see." Mum took the telegram and then she riffled through the others, her nose turning pink. "Who'd have thought he'd kept them all, all these years, all those border crossings?" she said. "He was a very sentimental man, my husband, a romantic at heart. Who'd have known?"

Dad had also kept his Post Office Savings Bank Book from 1958. He was just eighteen, and already on his way to becoming Tim Fuller of No Fixed Abode even then, scratching out his grandparents' address in York and replacing it with his father's address in Powys, Wales, then in turn scribbling out that address to replace it with an address in Londonderry, Northern Ireland.

"I didn't know Dad had lived in Ireland," I said.

"Not for long," Mum said. "Just to hide out from the aunts until he could flee the UK."

It had taken the man-boy who'd become my father a year to spend thirty-six pounds, fourteen shillings, and sixpence. At that point, the savings book zeroed out. It didn't make sense to me that of all things, my father would have kept a defunct savings book; the money was long spent and he was too much of a rule breaker to heed the warning, "KEEP THIS BOOK IN A SAFE PLACE. Its loss may cause you trouble."

But in the very last pages of the book, perhaps as a holdover from the world wars in which eighteen-year-old men were routinely shipped off to die, there was a page unapologetically headlined "Instructions for disposal of your income in the event of your death." Under this, my father had written clearly: "Have a party." I could almost hear him saying it, his signature cry when all else was lost. "Let's have a party!"

Tears had sprung to my eyes. "Look, Mum!"

Mum had taken the Post Office Savings Bank Book and clutched her throat. "Oh, Bobo. He'd known even then how he'd wanted to be seen off." Her eyes blazed. "Well, we won't let him down." She searched the room for the dogs. "Will we, Harry? Button? Coco?" Then she kissed the puppy cradled in her arms. "Will we, my Blue Duna?"

It was typical of my father, encouraging his bereaved friends and relatives to suffer spectacularly in the event of his death. Drinking was what you did when things were so overwhelmingly good you needed a hangover to tamp them down, or when things were so overwhelmingly bad you needed to forget. From that point of view, there was no reason not to get drunk at a memorial service; one of those things was bound to apply.

In the end, perhaps my father had held on to this old Post Office Savings Bank Book for practical reasons. Where else but in an old-fashioned bank ledger would he have been able to record his instructions for the disposal of his income in the event of his death? Online banking didn't make room for such a basic, but fundamentally important, question.

THE DAY OF THE MEMORIAL SERVICE DAWNED clear and still, eight days after Dad's death in Budapest, and a world away. We'd set the time for the service for the early afternoon, but from late morning villagers began to arrive and settle on the lawn in front of the pub at the bottom of the farm. Representatives from the Customs and Immigration Department, nurses from the Italian

Mission Hospital, neighboring farmers, and local fishermen silently congregated. Everyone wore black; most of the women had covered their heads with scarves.

"Oh, dear," Mum had said, taking her place front and center of the hushed gathering. "It is like a funeral, isn't it?" She wore a white silk blouse with large black dots on it, something a jockey might get away with, and a pair of black, light linen trousers, suitable for the heat. "Black is supposedly a forgiving color," Mum had observed desperately, brushing the dog hair off her knees. "Unless you're surrounded by a flock of Jack Russell terriers with mostly white coats."

We sat together; the family and the dogs, plus everyone Dad had mentioned in his final days—Mrs. Tembo, Mr. Chrissford, Mr. Kalusha, Comrade Connie—also a few people he'd forgotten about, or whom he'd willfully ignored. Vanessa's second son, the pregnant daughter-in-law, and the great-grandchild, they were with us. Serenity had dissolved in tears at the sight of Mum and had had to be removed to gaze upon tranquil scenes of banana leaves.

"I never see the point of small children at these things," Mum hissed at Vanessa. "Do you?" Mum had long ago declared her intention to forgo attending church until sensible rules had been set in place by the Archbishop of Canterbury if need be, or the Queen of England herself, for the disposal of unweaned and/or unruly children during services. "How are you supposed to observe the proper liturgies for special days when you're confronted with a dozen slurping Little Pig Robinsons and a whole bunch of howling little Serenities?"

Vanessa wore a blue tunic over blue palazzo pants; she had a long blue-and-white scarf wrapped around her neck and trailing behind her, much to the interest of Mum's Jack Russell terriers.

Isadora Duncan sprang to mind. "I tell you what, Al-Bo," Vanessa said, leaning over to me and speaking in a stage whisper. "I'm a total wreck. I don't know if I can take this." Mum glared at us. Vanessa popped one of Mum's knockout pills under her tongue and handed me one. "Mum thinks this is a dud batch," she said. "Do you think we should have two? I'd like to be wafting in the rafters, if possible."

After that there was a pause, as if we'd all inhaled collectively, but now none of us quite knew how to exhale, to start this ending. Then Vanessa's middle daughter, Megan, stood up and took center stage, in front of the pub's kitchen hutch. She sang "Jerusalem" a cappella. "And did those feet in ancient times," we'd all sung that enough over the years, on the roof of a Land Rover usually, Dad at the wheel.

Mum nodded approvingly, mouthed along as Megan sang, swayed a little from side to side. Mum adored Megan; Megan Nicola, she was the only one of the nine grandchildren who'd been named after her. Megan was fanatical about animals, and was very good with them, also she loved the farm, she was blindingly blonde, she read well, and was squeamish about anything to do with nudity and hugging. She disapproved of swearing, drugs, and anything else not wholesome and outdoorsy. She wasn't nosy and she didn't like nosy people. She was, in Mum's opinion, practically the perfect child.

"Megan would have been head girl of her junior school in Lusaka," Mum never tired of reminding anyone who'd listen. "The headmaster begged and begged for her to stay on; but Vanessa and Rich wanted to send her to South Africa." Mum had taken this blow personally. "Poor Megan. She'd have made a very good head girl. She's a star in the classroom. She's very athletic."

She could also sing like an angel; it was a lot to take, and very hard not to cry. William Blake's epic poem set to Sir Hubert Parry's music, piping out across the banks of the roiling Zambezi River. "Dark Satanic Mills," Mum warbled softly, a beat behind Megan. She'd issued stern warnings ahead of the memorial; there'd be no performances of any kind tolerated. She had been to those services, lots of wailing and shrieking. "Catholics are a proper sweat," she'd shuddered. "There's always lots of guilty secrets, mistresses howling like hyenas, illegitimate kids scattered all over the place looking murderous."

Megan took her place next to Mum; there was a round of applause, it was an ovation-worthy performance. Mum patted Megan's knee. "Oh, encore, my darling. Encore," she whispered. "That means 'once more' in French." Mum had been panicking about Megan's education, and supplementing it the way she'd supplemented ours, a sprinkling of French here, a smattering of Swahili there, an introduction to this opera, an obsession with Picasso, potted histories of everywhere, natural histories of everything. She'd been born with a vast, eclectic appetite for life; it was enough for three, it was enough for scores, it was enough for an army. She took Megan's victories and defeats personally. "Beautifully done," Mum assured Megan.

The applause died down. Then I'd stood in front of the kitchen hutch; the pub was like a small airplane hangar, it was designed to catch the breeze, not the eye of an editor at South Africa's *Garden and Home* magazine. The space still quivered with Megan's gorgeous song and with my father's sprit; he'd have loved it, and suddenly the plaintive fact of that conditional tense overwhelmed me. We'd never know for sure what my father would have felt or said about anything; certainty had been quenched.

Dad would have.

He would have.

It was like loving God, and then guessing what God would prefer. We'd never really know from now on, but from now on we'd all be striving for it and fighting over it. I could feel it already; each of us taking a stand behind the man we'd known, each feeling our knowing of him to be superior. The primacy of marriage, the importance of the oldest child, my incessant probing and processing; we'd all understood ourselves in relation to this man as if our understanding of him were central to our beings.

"Yes, well, you write very flatteringly of Dad," Mum had complained. "You've made him sound like Marcus Aurelius, all stoicism and bon mots, and you've made me sound like a racist alcoholic, forever oppressing the natives and swilling booze. Anyway, it's brandy, by the way, not whisky. You've written 'whisky.' That is inaccurate; I very rarely drink whisky."

Now, Mum was glaring at me intently. I cleared my throat and read a poem about love and a long marriage in honor of my parents. It wasn't something I had written myself, so Mum hadn't minded too much, although she'd stifled a yawn when the poem proved to have not only a third but also a fourth verse. "I was afraid you were never going to start, and then once you started I was afraid you were going to go on and on," she said under her breath when I sat back down.

After that, Rich gave a eulogy to celebrate Dad's life. Actually, it was mostly a list of notable fish caught by Rich as a result of having been introduced to fly-fishing by Dad. "Surprisingly, Rich loves fly-fishing," Mum had said. "Standing for hours and hours staring at the same little patch of water, who'd have thought God had the patience?" But Rich not only had the patience for fishing; his entire life revolved around it. He tied his own flies, he had built his house near a reservoir on a game farm, and he organized his family holidays around fishing.

"Very boring for moi," Vanessa whispered, leaning over me to roll her eyes extravagantly at Rich. But Rich wasn't deterred from the trajectory of his eulogy; he lovingly laid out details of the fishing expedition accompanying each notable fish caught, the bodies of water in which the fish had been found, the lure or fly used. He also made mention of the climatic conditions and alcohol consumed on the days in question. A lot of the fishermen at the service were riveted.

"Very suitable." Mum smiled and nodded when Rich sat down.

Then Mr. Chrissford had taken command of the space in front of the kitchen hutch. Boss Shupi had given Mr. Chrissford a tie to wear, on which there were small golden Zimbabwe birds, "to commemorate Mr. Fuller's ties on that side of the river," Boss Shupi had explained.

"Witty." I'd noticed.

Boss Shupi had nodded modestly. "Exactly."

Mr. Chrissford was solemn and venerable; he's always reminded me of an English village policeman taken straight from the pages of E. F. Benson's comic novels set in the fictitious 1930s Sussex town of Tilling. He rode a bicycle most places, even through the thick sand, sitting bolt upright and looking out at the bananas, the irrigation ditch, the fishponds. Also, while he appeared tolerant of everyone's foibles, there was a sense that we were each a single transgression away from being hauled in for a stern lecture. Mr. Chrissford was a serious man of God.

"All my top staff are very devout," Mum had told me. "Sundays are very depressing. Everyone goes creeping off to church and the farm is deadly silent except for the fish feeding. Any chaos I want I have to create for myself."

It was with some authority that Mr. Chrissford reminded us all that farmers require no introduction to God. Farmers are God's favorite children, because they are always asking for help. Hippos on the island off the bank gave a shout of agreement. We wiped our tears.

And finally, Hallelujah! Or the Hallelujah chorus from Handel's *Messiah*; we got to our feet, all of us, and did our best to sing that in his honor. Dad had performed in many pubs south of the equator, north of the Limpopo. It's a song, I find, that rewards a confident delivery; definitely something more easily done while drunk. Then a wind suddenly picked up and waves whipped up the Zambezi River, and for a moment we'd all turned and watched the water.

"That'll be Tim!" one of the old-timers shouted.

And it was over. Or it had just started. Or nothing had changed, but everything had begun again, without him. "Olé!" Mum shrieked. But for the first time in over half a century there was no answering echo. Mum put her arms up in the air. "Right," she said. "Someone rectify this drought! Music, maestro, music!" She took to the dance floor, her dogs in a circle around her.

"She's coping all right, isn't she?" Vanessa said.

"Yes, she's coping very well," I said.

People coped in different ways, Dad always said. And some people had more to cope with than others. Coping was the brave thing to do. Mum was doing the *very* brave thing.

IT WAS THE SMALL HOURS by the time Mum was carried to bed, feet first. But shortly after dawn, the drapes and curtains shook and her arms appeared, clutching a limp and apologetic Duna. "Bobo? Are you there? I'm afraid we've had a *little* accident," Mum said. I took the proffered puppy. "God, I feel rotten," Mum said.

"You were in bed nice and early. That's lucky. You'll have extra energy to fetch me tea."

"And a couple of aspirin?" I offered.

"Mm," Mum said. "Maybe. I'm having a bit of a religious experience this morning, as Dad would say."

"Dad would be proud of you," I said. "Very. You coped excessively well last night, I thought."

"Mm," Mum agreed modestly. "I did, didn't I?"

MY FATHER DRANK IMMODERATELY, but unlike Mum, he didn't drink immoderately only to cope. Nor did he drink wildly solely because he appreciated a decent thrash, although there was also that. Dad also occasionally drank to impressive excess because he said a proper hangover did wonders for the soul; it was one's spiritual duty. "It leaves a person filled with remorse and self-recrimination," Dad argued. "It's the quickest path to contrition."

My father suffered some monstrous hangovers in his time, obviously. He never hid the effects of a proper binge; he couldn't. He'd awaken the morning after the night before wearing only a dinner jacket and a wig, for example. "Oh, dear," he'd say. His lipstick would be smudged; there'd be bruises and injuries to the body.

"No, no, no," he'd protest weakly, staggering onto the veranda to greet the other survivors. "It wasn't me, it was my brother." He'd look around, survey the damage, wipe his eyes a few times in disbelief. "Dear God, you all look awful," he'd say. "Is there an official body count yet?"

Then he'd shave, dress in his working clothes, swallow a couple of aspirin with a cup of tea—his standard treatment for everything from a hangover to a heart attack—and reappear on the veranda, bleary but ready for the day's duty. "Right," he'd say, lighting a courageous cigarette. "That's quite enough buggering about for the time being. I am in the throes of a transcendentally painful hangover and I intend to use it well."

After that, he'd spend the day in the workshop, punishing himself under an old tractor, or welding the leak in a boiler. Or he'd go out on one of Mum's horses most of the day, sweating, shaking up his liver, cursing his pounding head, but determinedly cheerful and fatalistic too, as if he found his own terrible discomfort a duty to be endured lightly, a welcome metaphysical overhaul.

"Instead of church," he insisted. "A proper hangover makes you feel just as rotten as a good sermon should, but it saves a trip to town. It relieves the vicar from having to pretend he remembers you when it's perfectly obvious he'd never set eyes on you before. And it saves the church roof from getting hit by lightning."

CHAPTER THREE

Routine: Nature's Antidote
to Disappointment

Six months before my father died, I'd taken my eldest child out to Zambia as a part of her twenty-first-birthday present. "Surviving your grandparents on their own turf," I'd said. "It's the ultimate rite of passage."

Riot of passage, I'd been anticipating.

But from the moment they'd picked us up at the airport from the nine a.m. flight from Atlanta via O. R. Tambo, Mum and Dad had been on the best, most solicitous behavior of their lives.

"No, no, no," Dad said to Sarah, waving over porters to pick up our luggage. "Don't carry your own suitcases. You'll give yourself a hernia. Do you also travel everywhere with a complete library? Your grandmother does. Come on, chaps, fuga moto," he told the porters. "My granddaughter's come all the way from America." He returned his attention to Sarah. "Was it a terrible flight? Horribly bumpy? Crying babies? Cardboard eggs for breakfast? No champagne?"

"It was fine, Grandpa," Sarah said.

"Rubbish," Dad disagreed. "You have to sit with your knees

around your ears. The pilots aren't being paid enough to keep the damn thing airborne. And the airlines are very stingy with their hospitality these days; you have to marry the trolley dolly just to get a cup of tea. It's certainly not the service someone of your stature and class deserves." He bowed and scraped backward in front of Sarah like Mr. Nixon, to demonstrate the nonstingy hospitality he envisioned for her. "Perhaps you prefer grappa for breakfast, miss?" he said, in his best impression of an old English butler. "How about a little gunpowder in your tea? Of course you must have champagne, baths of it, fountains and rivers!"

We burst out of the clammy airport. It was the end of the rainy season. Lusaka was at its most generous; the floods had receded, the cholera clinics had closed for another year. The landscape was saturated, green, lush; there were white egrets everywhere. The trees were fruiting; mangos, papayas, guavas, like little loaves of ripening sunlight. Even Mum didn't need to point out how glorious everything was; it sang its own praises.

"I parked as close as I could," Dad said apologetically, mopping his brow, as the porters ferried our bags across the baking parking lot. "It's very taxing, this climate," Dad explained to Sarah. "For delicate people such as yourself. But don't worry, you'll be fine as soon as you have a couple of cold beers. Won't she, Tub?"

"Absolutely," Mum gushed, beaming. She hadn't taken her eyes off Sarah since we'd come rushing through Customs and Immigration toward the elderly couple waving at us, as if still directing the plane toward the gate. "Such a beautiful girl," Mum said. "Gorgeous eyes, skin like a peach. Don't you think she looks just like Grace Kelly? I think you look like Grace Kelly, or that other one. Drew something, the American actress."

Sarah blinked at me.

"You have wonderful bone structure," Mum was continuing,

pressing her fingers to her own cheeks. "You can't pay a plastic surgeon for bones. That's breeding."

"And here we are," Dad announced happily.

I looked around. I couldn't see the farm vehicle. My heart sank. It was gone. It was nowhere I could see. It had been stolen and Dad was senile, obviously, dreaming that all was well when all was clearly lost. Meantime, Mum was still grinning at Sarah like a fairy-story grandmother, by which I mean, hungrily.

"I don't see the car," I said.

"No, no, Bobo. Right here," Dad said, laughing; he made a gesture like a French waiter uncorking a fine wine in front of a brand-new Ford pickup. "Your chariot awaits," he said to Sarah. He opened the back door for Sarah, produced a cold, sweating beer from a cooler. "It's essential you drink a lot," Dad said. "But whatever you do, don't touch the water. I did once." He shook his head. "Bloody nearly fatal. Nasty stuff."

The porters packed our suitcases in the very back and tied everything down with nylon ropes; blue frayed nylon ropes, those had been with us always. For once there was plenty of room; no generator bleeding oil under a tarpaulin, no fish food exuding a fishy stench that no amount of scrubbing with Omo could dint, and there was no farm shopping.

"Put your feet up, put your feet up," Dad insisted. "What else can we offer you, Sarah?" Dad did a quick review of what he remembered of young people. It wasn't much. "I expect you want to go to the disco," he said at last.

The disco?

I shook my head at Sarah vehemently. Rashly, I'd taken my father up on that offer in Harare in the late 1980s, the year I'd been shipped off to secretarial college in the effort to make something useful of me. I'd been about the age Sarah was now. The disco was in Avondale, but beyond that I don't remember much about the evening, except that I awoke the next morning grateful to be alive. "Oh no," Dad had said, contrite too. "I don't remember much either. Perhaps we should wear dark glasses until we're sure the authorities aren't looking for us."

"No, really, Grandpa, thank you," Sarah said now. "But I need peace and quiet. I have to write my thesis."

That impressed my parents, I could tell.

"The-sis," Mum repeated slowly and clearly, as if hoping someone might overhear.

"Peace and quiet," my father mused uncertainly. They were new concepts to him, in a lot of ways, or reintroduced concepts. In any case, it wasn't what he was expecting from a grandchild, especially not one he was doing his best to lead astray in her twenty-second year, as is the duty of any right-thinking grandparent, but he recovered quickly. "Anything for you, Sarah. For you, we killa da cockroach," he said.

It was as if I'd been transported to a near replica of my parents' lives, creepily off in ways only I could feel, but that would have been hard to explain. These were my wonderful, exuberant parents; this was their glorious, hilarious life; these were their basic personalities brought up to bright burnish, but where was the assuaging bad behavior? Where were the sharp edges of these people? Where was the steady stream of minor shocks, aftershocks?

"No, no, no! There will be no shocks," Mum said, as if reading my mind, as usual. "Not with our most precious granddaughter here." She smiled at Sarah with terrifying reassurance. "You'll be fine. Grandpa's put in lots of extra practice with the shotgun. Not that we need it; he likes to keep his eye sharp, that's all." Mum smiled with terrifying assurance again, this time at her ankles, as if they'd been in agreement with her. "It's been simply ages since we had a rabid dog or anything, hasn't it, Hon?"

"Oh, weeks," Dad agreed.

Dad had only one eye, technically; or, only one working eye. He'd recently had laser eye surgery in Lusaka, but the whole thing had been so boring, and also expensive—"I had to show up sober as a judge first thing in the morning, and lie there without complaining or scratching my nose while they emptied the contents of my bank account," Dad had said—that he'd refused to get the other eye done, vowing to train Harry as a seeing-eye dog before he'd subject himself to such horror again. "I have a pretty consistent routine," he'd said. "Round the bananas, down to the pub, up to the fishponds. It'd be a piece of cake for Harry."

We jolted out of the airport. Dad didn't have his usual argument with the tollbooth keeper about the unmarked speed bumps, and about how they always took him by surprise and at his age surprises can be fatal; he did not want to die in the parking lot of Kenneth Kaunda International Airport. Nor did he go into the injustice to the public of the escalating cost of airport parking. "Does it look like I'm made of money?" he always wanted to know.

But now he did look as if he were made of money. He said so himself. "Don't we look posh?" he asked the tollbooth keeper, handing him a fresh twenty-kwacha bill. "Keep the change. Don't spend it *all* on women and wine. Spare some change to have a flutter on the game. Who's your team? The Dynamos?"

"I'm for the Red Arrows, Bwana," the tollbooth keeper said.

"Pamberi Red Arrows!" Dad agreed.

Then we swept off down the airport road. Chinese contractors had recently paved it over; it gleamed black and smooth. The flame trees lining the road were dropping fat red blooms. Cattle on either side of the road shone in belly-deep pasture. The pickup was white, there were no dents in it; the windscreen had not yet suffered the usual indignities of a Zambian vehicle. We were like the living embodiment of a William Carlos Williams poem.

"Special order," Dad said proudly, thumping his fist on the steering wheel. "All the bells and whistles." The pickup had manual locks, manual mirrors, crank windows, *and* air-conditioning. Dad had put a new blanket from the Chirundu market on the backseat; it still smelled of the bale it had arrived in from India. There wasn't even a humiliated, vomiting dog on anyone's lap.

"Do you have enough room back there?" Mum asked Sarah; she sounded genuinely anxious, perhaps because she'd made such an ostentatious fuss of cranking her seat so far forward she was now mere inches from the pickup's passenger airbag. "Are you comfortable?" she asked. "Is the wind too much?"

Is the wind too much?

I shook my head at Sarah in disbelief. "Never," I said. "It was *never* like this when I was a kid." In the end I decided Sarah was being rewarded because she, like Megan, the other poster grandchild, was everything Mum had wished for in her own children. "You have such lovely manners," Mum told Sarah. "You're *so* kind." Mum said, "So kind," like the queen, *sew koind*. "Did you also have to get your teeth all wired up? Americans have to wire up their teeth, don't they?"

"Yes," Sarah said.

"Well, you can't tell," Mum said approvingly. And it was clear that Mum was pleased that although Sarah was of childbearing age, she'd managed, unlike Vanessa's second son, to remain childless. Mum brought that up a couple of times too, casually slotting it into conversation. "Yes, your cousin does seem to have gotten off the mark rather hotfoot." And, "I do think it makes sense to travel while you're still young. Before you have children." Also,

"It's not fashionable to have children until you're at least thirty these days, is it?"

We stopped at the Rock on the way down, as usual. Mr. Nixon scurried out from the kitchen to offer us tea. "Tell the madam we're here," Mum said, as she always did. Mr. Nixon backed off the veranda one limb at a time, smiling graciously. I'd tried to explain my family's culture to my children; I'd written books about my childhood and my mother's in part because I wasn't sure how else they'd ever know their Zambian-resident grandparents, their Anglo-Zambian aunt. "It's like a mash-up of a whole lot of Meryl Streep movies," I'd said at last. "'A dingo's got my baby' and *Out of Africa*, except with more cats."

After a while, Mr. Nixon returned with a tray of tea, and then Vanessa wafted out of her bedroom onto the veranda with a Persian under each arm. She was wearing dark glasses. "Migraine," she explained, distributing exhausted air kisses all round. "Rich was snoring all night." Then she'd turned her attention to Sarah. "Are you sure you want to go to the farm?" she said. "Nastasya was nearly decapitated in the library a few years ago."

BUT THIS WASN'T THAT VISIT: My parents had done up the guest cottage especially for Sarah. Shade cloth had been pinned under the tin roof to help mitigate the heat and insects, a couple of floor fans from the Chirundu market stirred the warmth about a bit. "Quite safe," Mum boasted. "You'd need to wrench off the grille and stick your head in the blades to do yourself any harm with a fan like this. Made in China too, so it's probably quite feeble. I mean if it was your whole head versus one little floor fan."

"Mum!" I said.

"I'm just saying," Mum said. "After all the fuss Vanessa's made about Nastasya and the library fan. It didn't nearly decapitate her. She was in the room and it plopped out of the ceiling. No one was hurt. Not even a dog, and they're everywhere."

There were signs that the undergrowth had been recently thinned, the jungle hacked back a bit. "I went through the whole place with a fine-tooth comb," Mum said, showing Sarah to her room. "And I had a long conversation with all the creatures I met, explaining you're American. I asked them to behave, or to leave the premises. For your maximum, tip-top, worry-free enjoyment." She smiled ingratiatingly at Sarah, expectantly, like a hotel porter awaiting a tip.

"Thank you so much, Granny," Sarah said. "It's perfect."

"Do you really think so?" Mum said. She looked around the guest cottage with pride, as if seeing it for the first time, its delights and wonders. "I put the finishing touches to it myself," she said.

She pointed out the little bottles of shampoo and conditioner taken from hotels long ago and saved for a very special occasion; those were in the bathroom. "There's only cold water," Mum said. "I can't get your grandfather to stretch to hot water for the guests, he thinks that might encourage riffraff."

Also, there wasn't much Mum could do about the frogs, skinks, geckos, centipedes, and insects that had managed to sneak in through the wide-open veranda, and the bits below the tin roof where the shade cloth had run out. "They don't do any harm," Mum said. "But we always shake out our towels and shoes. Just a precaution, nothing to worry about."

She showed Sarah the table where she'd left the sorts of books any young person might enjoy—volumes of Agatha Christie's mysteries, *The Burgess Bird Book for Children* by Thornton W. Burgess, and an old copy of H. E. Marshall's 1905 *Our Island Story*. Everything was smothered in Blue Death.

"I know you'd never lick your fingers to turn the pages," Mum said, but she'd glanced at me as if not trusting my parenting skills to have extended as far as they should. "People who do, and who borrow my books, have reported feeling sick." Mum paused to let this sink in for a moment. "From the Blue Death," she clarified. "Apparently it makes their throats close up." Mum paused again. "Whoever borrowed my copy of *My Life Was a Ranch* must not be a finger licker," she said, giving me a knowing look. "Or I'd have been blamed for their near death by now."

To this day, I know I remain one of two chief suspects in the filching of this esteemed memoir; the other being an ex-neighbor from thirty years ago who is now about eighty, maybe older, and who can't remember my mother, let alone borrowing a book from her. I think Vanessa has the book, though, stashed away with all her Beatrix Potters. "It's not Vanessa," Mum said if I ever brought up this line of defense. "She doesn't read anything except *Hello!* and South Africa *Fairlady*."

At supper that night my parents sat in rapt awe and admiration as they asked Sarah to describe in detail the premise of the thesis she was working on. They had to be told the title more than once: "The Role of Women in Revolution in Mexico and Cuba." "Oh, I love that idea!" Mum cooed. "No one thinks of women in combat, but they can be very useful." Mum blinked at me in meaningful reproach. "Very protective, and very accurate. May I read what you've written?"

By breakfast the next morning, Mum had read the entire thing twice. "Oh, it's very good," she said to Sarah. Sarah was battling her way through a plate of food—eggs, bacon, toast, bananas, papaya, lemons—larger than her head; my father had declared a terror she'd float away otherwise. "It's quite brilliant, really. You're a very good writer." Mum glanced at me. "Very good. Not everyone has your natural talent. You could write for a career if you wanted. Maybe you should?"

On the strength of this startlingly good review of her work, Dad had taken Sarah to the pub to join him for his elevenses after breakfast. He insisted she drive the new Ford down to the bottom of the farm, as a treat. "Go as fast as you like," he exhorted. When it became obvious she wasn't accustomed to a stick shift, Dad offered to change gears for her. All Sarah had to do was press the clutch and yell "Gear!"

At the pub, Dad made it clear that he assumed Sarah had come to Zambia with the primary goal of remaining in a mild alcoholic fog the entire time. "My usual, please, Shupi, and let me introduce you to my granddaughter. It's your job to make sure the picanin madam doesn't die of thirst under our watch."

A round of drinks was ordered and poured. Boss Shupi turned up the music. Harry bossed around the resident Jack Russell terriers, but he was in too good a mood to battle them off the guests' chairs, the way he usually did. Instead, he stood at the edge of the pub and greeted the hippos.

"Your very good health!" Dad toasted.

Everyone raised glasses. Someone asked what Sarah did in America.

"I'm a student," Sarah said.

"She's a suffragette," Dad said.

"I'm studying political science," Sarah explained.

"The lesbian parade," Dad clarified. "We're very, very proud."

Sarah blinked at Dad.

"Right!" Dad said, seeing the conversation was in danger of

stalling out. "Let's have a party!" I'd predicted this moment, at least. I'd warned Sarah never to try keeping up with my parents when it came to partying; dancing on bars, coercing would-be nondrinkers, breaking curfews, even military ones, these had been my parents' specialties their entire lives. "Drink up!" Dad told Sarah. "That'll put hairs on your chest."

WE WERE THERE THREE WEEKS; in retrospect, I'd have stayed longer. I'd have stayed until Dad died and until Mum was over the shock. In my ideal world, I'd have stayed on even then; I'd never have left the farm. In my ideal world, my three children would leave America and live with us, Vanessa's children too; I wouldn't have to choose between the generations and neither would my parents.

In my ideal world, my children's American father could visit, a tent or guest cottage of his own at the bottom of the garden; he'd always preferred a spot of his own where he could dream. In my ideal world, we'd never have divorced; it wasn't out of the question here, the farm threw people together. It had been my parents' secret to a long marriage, or part of it; they always had something larger than themselves to focus on, there was always chaos to keep at bay, they didn't bore each other, or bore through each other.

In my ideal world, the farm would pass down from one bunch of people to the next, from Mr. Chrissford and Mrs. Tembo and Comrade Connie to their children, and their children's children; all of us meeting under the Tree of Forgetfulness next to the outdoor kitchen for meals, and always, a new generation of dogs under the table, waiting for morsels.

And if that's what we'd wanted, Dad had given us all a place to call home as long as you didn't need too much comfort, as long as you were happy with cold water, no walls, and the constant busy intrusion of life, tumbling, insistent, demanding life. In the end, he'd done that for Mum and for anyone who'd tolerate his brand of existence: gritty and hilarious, spontaneous and hard won, chaotic and routine.

"Someone will have to deal with the pensions office when I'm gone," Dad had said. His strategy had been to hide when they came around, or he sent Harry out to greet them, with Mum. "Too bad they show up in posh four-wheel-drive SUVs," Mum said. "Instead of bicycles. It would be tactful if they did show up on bicycles. It would prove they weren't siphoning off the funds, and it would give Harry an incentive to go after them, wouldn't it, Harry?"

Dad, having learned to his personal cost what happened to money once the Zambian government had managed to garner it, couldn't be moved to comply with the pension scheme. "But it's a nationwide scheme, Mr. Fuller," the pension people from Lusaka had pointed out.

"Comrade Fuller to you," Dad had replied coldly. "And when I see a single kwacha of these funds going toward the working povo in the rural areas, and not toward the fat cats in the city, I will happily contribute the hard-won funds of my fellow comrades to your scheme, but not until then."

Dad had tailor-made the place for Mum, it was easy to see now: There was the pub at the bottom of the farm, and an ongoing battle with the pensions officers, it gave a person reason to drink. There was a wild tangle of garden, in which dogs could roam, snakes and lizards could sunbathe, wild monkeys could clatter and shriek. And there was a brand-new Ford pickup. "They keep going for years," Dad assured Sarah. "Not like computers. Have you heard of built-in obesity? Is that what it's called? It's an idea invented by the Chinese and perfected by that computer bloke who wants to castrate us all. Shupi can tell you all about it."

There were three meals a day; tea all day, baths before dinner, two walks with the dogs. There was weeding in the bananas, harvesting; the fish were fed morning and afternoon. The farm's schoolchildren left the compound for their lessons at dawn, their chattering like so many birds. We missed them until late afternoon, when they returned from school to shoot pigeons at Mum's ponds with homemade catapults; that always gave everyone their afternoon exercise, Mum chasing after the schoolchildren, the schoolchildren taunting the dogs, the dogs having an uproarious time. Life churned on and on and took us all with it.

"Routine," Dad said. "It's nature's antidote to disappointment." After dinner, accordingly, he insisted Sarah go to the fishponds, crocodile shooting. "Every evening before bed," Dad said. "It settles the digestion to take a potshot at your enemies." So Sarah held the flashlight and tried to direct it toward anything that looked like two red eyes gleaming back from the water.

"Don't worry," Dad reassured Sarah. "I hardly ever manage to hit anything, you're quite safe." The shotgun was Turkish, a terrible weapon with a kick like a mule, and the sights didn't line up with Dad's one working eye. Also, crocodiles are very smart. "We didn't need the Frog Croc Bird to tell us that," Dad said. "They have a very good brain, they can easily outthink a white man any day."

Mum's dogs hopped and barreled ahead of us, flinging themselves into the fishponds. "Just to give the crocodiles fair warning," Dad explained. Then there was a whole performance while the dogs were persuaded to get out of the line of fire. Sarah shone the light on the pond; it wasn't easy to stop the Jack Russell terriers from going after the beam. Then seemingly randomly Dad fired off a couple of shots in quick succession.

"Oh, missed again," Dad said. "Never mind. Better luck next time." Then he held the cracked shotgun over his forearm, staring up at the moon for a moment, a silver sliver tonight, waxing crescent. Shooting stars rained down through a sky so black it looked like a time before time. "Right, Harry. What do you say? Should we call it a night?" So we'd all called it a night; we'd taken a crack at the enemy of the fish farmer, and we all felt better for it, our digestion settled, our routine honored.

I LOVED THOSE NIGHTS in the guest cottage, Sarah in the room next to mine. Dogs sprinting between our beds, looking for the best deal, the most room under a mosquito net. Insects buzzed and battered against the security lights. They rained down onto the concrete floor, their little bodies clattering.

The tin roof heaved and sawed in the wind. Frogs chorused in the wetland between the house and the bananas. Short, scuffling disagreements broke out among the vervet monkeys roosting in the Tree of Forgetfulness. The Jack Russell terriers Mum had thrown into bed with me burrowed under the sheet. "Have a couple of dogs, Bobo," Mum had always said when she was tucking me into bed. She didn't trust everything to Blue Death. "Sleep tight."

Perhaps this was the childhood my parents had been aiming for, when they'd envisioned raising children in southern and central Africa. They'd so nearly got it perfectly right. We'd had this happy chaos, a lot of it; we had a world of endless pets. Our beds were smothered like William Morris wallpaper, a friendly face poking out from behind the fronds of our mosquito nets.

There had been wide-open spaces; we'd had music when the

generator was on. We'd had a library stuffed with books that Mum had harvested from fleeing white families over the years; raked out of secondhand bookstores. As a matter of routine, we'd been encouraged to read the sorts of books that are supposed to enrich, entertain, and evolve us. *Our Island Story* was such a classic; David Cameron had cited it as one of his favorites.

Mum's shoulders slumped when I'd told her this news. "But he's so boring," she complained; David Cameron was not Mum's idea of properly conservative. He was nouveau right wing; a laddish, overgrown schoolboy, she thought. She hadn't even named a dog after him. She'd had a Maggie, a Winston, and a Boris. She'd even had an Aung San Suu Kyi—"House arrest did wonders for her complexion," Mum had observed at the time—but never a David Cameron.

I'd had that mother growing up; articulate, impossible, strong, and sometimes so wrong she was right, but not always. Sometimes she was just wrong, but it didn't devastate her, or not for long. She'd marched on anyway, and in the meantime she'd shored us up, comforted us with dogs, inspired us with art, stunned us with her own life's brilliant performance. She was an act to follow, a flame to read by, she was a fighter.

"Mum will be okay," Dad told me one night on that visit; a mellow moment before dinner, Mrs. Tembo teaching Sarah how to make rice in the kitchen, Mum in the bath catching up on world news. "She likes a bit of a challenge; she loves a proper dustup. I'm a natural coward. I'd far prefer to hide under the bed, but your mother . . ." Astonishingly, Dad's eyes had suddenly welled. "She's stronger than anyone I know. Remember that, Bobo. Your mother is a survivor. She makes it look easy." He shook his head in wonder. "She makes it look like a piece of cake."

A solid sense of dread hit the top of my stomach. I knew then

I wouldn't be back here. Or some part of me knew Dad was telling me what I needed to know for the road ahead, because he wouldn't be here much longer. He must have known he'd soon be a shadow along that road, and then some few months and a day later, not even that.

"The routine will carry Mum along, Bobo," Dad said. "And once she gets her sea legs under her, you just watch her sail! The farm will turn record profits when I finally pop my clogs. You mark my words."

CHAPTER FOUR

A Widow's Farm

Mum never tires of telling anyone who'll listen, and some who won't, and still others who don't care, that she's the majority shareholder on the farm. "Not everyone realizes, I'm the majority shareholder on the farm," she explains. She doesn't exactly throw her weight around, that would be unseemly and exhausting, but after so many years of unrecognized toil, she's making sure to get a bit of the spotlight for once.

"Dad had the idea for the farm," she says, giving credit where credit is due. "He had the flash of inspiration, and the energy to stagger down here week after week to negotiate with the headman, but I had the *bucks* for it." Mum thinks "bucks" sounds filthy rich, like an American. She uses the word when she's being deliberately vulgar, which it always is to talk about money except surprise money, insignificant-seeming money, incidental money, you could mention that, sort of.

"Egg money," Mum used to call it when there was a little spare cash; that was when she had lived on farms with more chickens and fewer snakes. Or "Cheapie-sale money," Mum said of the days when you could still competitively sell your shabby worn-out clothing to people even less well-off than you. That had been during the era of Kenneth Kaunda's so-called Zambian humanism; everyone had been cash-strapped back then.

"At least everyone was poor together," I'd argued. I should have known better. I'd costarred in my high school's adaptation of George Orwell's *Animal Farm*; I'd played Snowball to Amelia Davidson's Napoleon. Mum, who'd come to nearly all my school performances—"Bobo needs a dramatic outlet; she has an overactive imagination"—had boycotted this one on the grounds she was a current victim of Marxist-Leninist politics, and didn't need to have her nose rubbed in it by the kids at my posh private boarding school in Harare.

"No, I'm not nostalgic for socialism, Bobo," Mum had said. "It was a heck of a strain for those of us making it easier for the rest of you. Dad can live off baked beans, tobacco, and tea for months and claim to enjoy the weight loss. But someone still has to wrestle open the baked beans and serve them by Chinese-made paraffin candlelight. Someone had to come up with the fees for your posh private boarding schools. No, the novelty of poverty wore off for me a long, long time ago."

She knew all the lyrics, or at least the chorus, to quite a few songs about money. Above all, she loved Tevye the Dairyman's famously rousing reverie, "If I Were a Rich Man," from Sheldon Harnick and Jerry Bock's 1964 *Fiddler on the Roof*; she'd seen the musical performed at Reps Theatre in Harare. She'd bought the video starring Chaim Topol as Tevye, and watched it until the wasps' nest in the VCR had put an end to that.

"The problem with your father and money," Mum had said, "one of them, is that he's prone to get overexcited whenever he has any. He lays it on with a trowel for everyone: champagne, escargot, cigars, then we're back to starvation rations and panic over your school fees. Not that I minded the sacrifice." She gave me a quick, sour look. "It was worth *every* bead of sweat and blood." It's true Mum had strained every sinew—she'd literally scalded her hands in vaults of fermenting eggplants; she'd rustled cattle—to get the money together to send us to the best schools possible. Anyway, it wasn't the cost of our education that bothered Mum so much as what Vanessa and I had done with it; my Awful Books, Vanessa's artistic rendition of Edvard Munch's *The Scream*. We'd been given the best start possible, and behaved ungratefully in return.

Vanessa and I had been educated with politicians' kids; the Zimbabwean minister of transport's exceedingly young wife was in the form ahead of me; royalty went to our schools; so did the children of wealthy white farmers. "Bobo's been affecting a posh accent ever since Form One," Mum explained.

At the beginning and end of term, and during the half-term break, the politicians' chauffeurs arrived in Mercedes-Benzes with tinted windows. The rich white farmers were in Mercedes-Benzes without tinted windows. Everyone acted like they owned the place. Mum and Dad always arrived memorably and late; belching diesel fumes in the 1967 Land Rover with the back door swinging open and dogs plopping out onto the school driveway, seething around the parking lot.

"Well, at least we're not like everyone else," Mum said approvingly, looking around at the fleet of Mercedes-Benzes; black and white were the two most popular colors. Our dogs leapt up on people's gleaming paintwork. "Oh, dear, is that a run in my stocking?" Mum would become preoccupied with ignoring the chaos around her. Dad would light a cigarette and look the other way.

We had dogs, not bucks; we'd never have bucks. The kids at my school had bucks and dogs and also racehorses and sailboats.

Some of them had ski holidays in Europe, trips to the Alps, but they'd learned to wear it all lightly, or at least with casual entitlement. They were the expectant inheritors of land and power from their parents; no one talked about the wars that had gone on in pursuit of that land and power, although that war hadn't left us, I can see that now. It was in our fragility, our anorexia nervosa, our confusion. It was in the manner in which we averted our gaze from the discomfort and chaos and destruction we were causing.

I went back a few years ago to the school, five years before Dad died; twenty-five years after I'd left. The children of the political classes were there still, but the white farmers' kids were nearly all gone. Instead, there were the children of Chinese entrepreneurs; they were driving themselves to school, or being driven by chauffeurs, they now acted as if they owned the place. "The Chinese own Zimbabwe?" Mum had said when I'd commented about this shift in power. "That must be nice for them."

I hadn't been able to tell if she'd meant it.

VANESSA AND I WEREN'T EVER going to be heritage children. We would never *own the place*, not in the traditional gold-watch-and-portfolio sense of the word. It hadn't been planned this way; but it was the natural order of things, our end in our beginning. We were the murderous, murdered Orphans of the Empire, the stubborn remnants of a briefly glutted people; we were the half-life of our white supremacist violence, the aftershock of colonialism.

We belonged nowhere here; we belonged nowhere else.

Our rootlessness had brought with it a longing for belonging; Vanessa had always dreamed of an English country cottage with roses, I'd hankered to be born into village life, into community, a commune anywhere at all. "Rubbish," Mum had said. "You are

American now. What are you saying about commune? Every American needs at least one dedicated, private bathroom per bottom." She said "bathroom" the way she said "American," as if it indicated an automatic territoriality and an unfortunate predilection for saving extra space for oneself, like a German on a beach holiday.

Mum had garnered a couple of tiny inheritances from her family; there was the Scottish relative who had made her trip to London's West End possible. And her mother had left her a little money. "Very modest," Mum always said; but her inheritances had helped her become majority shareholder on the farm. Dad's family had overlooked him deliberately. It had embittered him for a long time. "They hang it over your head, even if there's nothing left to pass down," Dad had told me. "It's handcuffs if you look at it properly, not an inheritance."

Or everyone inherits something. None of us walks away unburdened; even the abandoned among us inherit rejection; the meek inherit it all. My parents had inherited the rickety scaffolding of an empire; they'd inherited a violent dismantling. Vanessa and I were inheritors of something much harder to put into words. We'd been shocked to the quick at the speed and intensity of our young lives; we'd been blinded with fear and loss and we'd been stoic, tough, and resilient.

Or they'd been stoic, tough, and resilient. Mum and Dad had been; they'd withstood, they'd borne up, they'd come back from defeat and humiliation; they'd turned from their failures and their tragedies and they'd faced the music more than once. "That's a bit of an understatement," Dad had said. "Your mother was practically conducting the orchestra."

That was Vanessa's and my inheritance. If we got nothing else from Mum and Dad, we knew how to face the music. They'd showed us how; we'd seen it done over and over, not easy music to face. They'd lived out of bounds all their lives, my parents; they'd made historic mistakes for which they'd paid cosmically and they'd endured in spite of it.

"Did I do this to get into one of your Awful Books?" Dad had asked from his deathbed in Budapest; lucidly present in the world I recognized for a moment.

I'd laughed then. "Probably."

Dad had chuckled too. "That'll annoy Mum."

Another Awful Book, how many more can be written?

Everyone in my family hates the books I write, they ask me to stop, but I can't look away. "Write novels," Dad begged, but real life never stops coming at me, and it pours from my pen more easily than fiction. It's not only the old adage to write what I know, but also to write what I love. And it's the artist's impulse to turn again and again to the same subject until the subject gives up its secrets. I can't pretend to know anyone's secrets, people are complicated, but I've stared and stared at the material. I know something, or some things.

I know Mum and Dad have come so far, too fast; they've stripped themselves bare again and again in their race through time and space; they've burned like asteroids, and crashed smoldering into other people's lives. But they've arisen again and again from the ashes, wiped their faces, turned and picked up the baton to call the string section to heel, and carried on with the show.

"Of course the show must go on," Mum always said.

The show went on, and on. There were reruns.

What a ride it had been, and what a perfect finish!

I mean the farm was the perfect finish, a magnificent flourish at the end of a full life. My father had dreamed this place into reality for my mother, and in turn my mother loves this farm. It's hers, and it nourishes her; it's her *nostalgie de la boue* satisfied.

What solace.

On quiet nights, you can sometimes hear lions roaring from the Zimbabwean side of the river, hyenas laughing, jackals yelping. Hippos often come up to the lawn in front of the pub to graze at night; in any case, they'd dispensed with the need for a mower. "Careful not to walk up a hippo's arse in the dark," Dad always warned if I left my barstool to venture into the pub's ablution block.

Occasionally in the dry season, elephants flicked through the electric fence and raided the bananas. In the early days, Dad always leapt out of bed to save the plantation. "It's not unheard of for people to get trampled," Mum had said at the time. "And there's your father skipping about in the dark wearing nothing but his kikoi and armed only with a cooking pot and a walking stick, up against five elephants." She'd sniffed, "I kept the dogs safely with me, and I said 'Cheerio' to Dad. 'I hope you come back unscathed.' But I didn't hold my breath. What a performance!"

THE PUB AND THE WILD GARDEN and the promise of reliable enemies, all that, of course, was a part of the wondrous life Dad had envisioned for Mum, but on top of this my father had decided to start fish farming. That had been a stroke of genius too, a finicky game in which thousands of creatures must be carefully watched over; fish are easily stressed, they're susceptible to every disease and parasite you can think of, and then things you couldn't imagine.

"Perfect for your mother," Dad had said.

"I've had to supplement my already overwhelming pile of reading," Mum had complained happily. "It's impossible to keep up with all the homework I must do." She'd added to the pile of things she needed to wade through by breakfast the most recent scientific and aquaculture papers. "Terribly technical, and a slog for the brain in this heat, but I do it, and I retain every word," Mum had said; she passed her reading on to Mr. Chrissford.

"Effects of Stocking Density on Growth of *Tilapia nilotica* Cultured in Cages in Ponds" by Antonio E. Carro-Anzalotta and Andrew S. McGinty. "Studies on the Feeding of the *Tilapia nilotica* in Floating Cages" by R. D. Guerrero III. They sounded like Mum's kind of men, going by the names alone, exotically foreign, probably wine drinkers, fish experts. Every morning, in the sanctuary of her bed, Mum's eyes are fixed on the pages of her homework, her hand reaching through the drapes for cups of tea, a couple of dogs at her feet.

"Your mother is like a very good horse," Dad had told me. "She needs a job, or she tends to kick the stable down a bit." Also, Dad had known Mum would grow the most spectacular fish possible because she loves all animals, and doing what you love sets you free, or it returns you briefly to the wholeness from which we believe ourselves torn. Mum is the most successful fish farmer in the whole of Zambia.

"Well, I don't know if I'd go *that* far," Mum said. Then she lifted her eyes at me and gave me a look of mild reproach that suggested she'd rather hoped I'd go a bit further. Mum loves her fish, and in turn they flourish. They rush to greet her, a tiny tidal wave of silver fins slicing the water's surface when she takes her thrice-daily walk around the ponds to check on them. "Oh, hello, my darlings," Mum purrs.

Their scales shimmer like bits of silver.

Dad had ensured the most miraculous thing for Mum in her golden years, her reluctant great-grandmother years. He'd brought her full circle back to the thrilling vibrancy of her perfect childhood. She'd hankered for it ever since he'd torn her from it on their wedding day, Mum's foot still dragging on the gravel as they'd raced off from their wedding reception. "I'll never understand why your father is in such a hurry all the time," my grandmother had complained.

But his impulsiveness refined over time toward spontaneity; his toughness resolved toward tenacity; his exuberance softened into humor. This farm was his final lasting gesture of love to Mum. He'd made her a home in the great, roiling, storied Zambezi Valley, and in so doing he'd brought her back to the home she'd never really left.

Or it was a hotter, denser, chattier place than her cool Kenyan highland youth, but it had all the markings of colonials gone mad, and that was the country Mum had never really left. The wild, intoxicating effects of her mother's homemade wine, the headiness of the thin air, the addicting idea that her station gave her automatic privilege; she'd never completely shed any of it.

"The Huntingfords had apparently dispensed with the distinction between inside and outside." Dad had told me this about meeting his future family-in-law for the first time. "There weren't walls, just some hessian sacks tacked up between planks. A gnat's fart would have blown the place down."

There were dogs everywhere, Dad had said of that rambling little farmhouse on the edge of Eldoret. Dairy cows wandered into the kitchen licking their nostrils in that luxuriating, repetitive way contented cows have. There was always a kitten or a wild mongoose recovering from something in a cardboard box by the Dover stove. There were horses nudging the flimsy windows off their hinges in search of a scratch, or a treat. "Then you go to bed, only to find tomorrow's breakfast, and possibly lunch, clucking away at the end of your bed," Dad had said. "It was absolute bloody mayhem."

It had taken two-thirds of their life together, but eventually my father had allowed Mum's love for absolute bloody mayhem to take root. But because it was also everything Mum knew in her blood and bones, it worked for her. It nourished her, all of it; it breathed life into her.

Even after Dad was dead, the farm had continued to roll with the seasons, as if he'd really gone nowhere and as if he really was everywhere; his crazy-healing dream scattered across that difficult, gorgeous piece of land. And with the farm's staff living across a narrow road from the dissolving farmhouse, with the constant lively companionship of animals, there'd be no chance Mum could ever be lonely. "Ever," Mum emphasized, rolling her eyes in exaggerated exhaustion. "I try to hide behind my drapes with the dogs to get some rest, but there's always someone knocking on the door, needing me for this and that."

FOR FOUR MONTHS AFTER HE DIED, Dad's ashes sat in the bomb casing on the bottom of Vanessa's bookshelf, next to her complete set of Beatrix Potter's children's books. "We can't put it off forever," I'd argued, calling Mum on the farm from my home in Wyoming. "We need to have a funeral, or burial, or a scattering, or whatever, sooner or later."

"But I haven't decided where to bury him yet," Mum had said.

"He said we were supposed to put a match to him, and then scatter the remains under the nearest tree," I'd said.

"Did he?" Mum had sounded doubtful. "I didn't hear him say anything like that."

"Well, he certainly didn't say, 'Put me on the bottom of Vanessa's bookshelf next to Jeremy Fisher and Peter Rabbit with the cats,'" I'd said.

"Mm," Mum had agreed. "It is very difficult to get anything back once it's landed on one of Vanessa's bookshelves." She'd paused. "You don't think she has my copy of *My Life Was a Ranch*, do you?"

"I have no doubt," I'd said.

But we'd never get proof. Ever since returning from the clinic in KwaZulu-Natal, and especially since submitting to the influence of Bindi, and increasingly since Dad had died, Vanessa's bedroom had become her castle; it was her fortress. Honestly, it was a minute private kingdom perched on the edge of a rock. She had an en suite bathroom, a walk-in closet, bookshelves, a view of the hills, a bed like a huge nest. Mum and I were green with envy.

"No one can come in here," Vanessa had said. To help with the problem of unannounced or unwanted visitors, Vanessa had taken to locking her bedroom door when she wasn't there, and even when she was. Only Mr. Nixon was welcome to bring in trays of tea, and clean out the cats' litter boxes. "I have to lock my door," Vanessa had said. "Otherwise things have a habit of growing legs and walking out of here."

It was true that both Vanessa and Mum had developed a habit of going in search of what they'd lost to each other, and failing to find it, replacing it with other interesting things they'd found. For decades, books and videos and even children's stuffed animals had been ferried secretively under tea towels or in diaper bags from the Rock to the farm and back again.

"I'll ask Rich to bring down the ashes to the farm," I'd finally offered. "If we don't do it now, we'll never do it."

"Mm," Mum had agreed.

The day we chose to scatter Dad's ashes was a working day, the farm bustling with a new year's fresh resolve. "We should get on with it first thing, before it gets too hot," Mum had said. But none of us could quite manage dawn, mostly because our chosen minister for the funeral, or burial, or whatever we were having, was an American artist with whom I was madly in love. We were engaged to be married, he was the opposite of me in many ways; I'd considered this a good thing.

"Well, yes," Mum had agreed. "That is a good thing. One of you is plenty."

Wen took the enjoyment of life seriously. He took fine food and good drink seriously, he grew his own fresh vegetables and knew his way around a wine list; he took art seriously, he labored over colors. He was attracted to Eastern philosophies, but he'd not become a man of the cloth seriously. He'd done it to officiate a friend's wedding at which there'd been buckets of strong margaritas; he'd received his ministerial certification online in seven minutes.

"Mm," Mum had said. "On my father's side, there was an Episcopalian bishop; my grandfather was a reverend. It was seven years of Greek and Latin; they were very cerebral and spiritual."

But Wen didn't have seven years of hard religious learning in him. He didn't prefer being awake too early the way a real priest does, he needed sleep. He took the research on the health effects of sleep seriously. He was very healthy, vibrant with life, easily thrilled by the simple joys of a stellar digestion, a good night's rest. "You're a lifetime of tired," he was always telling me. "You need to rest more, relax more." Wen took rest and relaxation very seriously. I'd loved that about him to begin with; the way he'd loved my excessive energy to begin with.

"He lives in a yurt," I'd warned Vanessa.

"A yacht?" she'd said.

"No, a yurt."

Vanessa told everyone he lived in an igloo. After I showed her his art, she pronounced us the groovy couple; she adored Wen's whimsical style. "He looks very young," she'd said when I'd sent a photo. I'd had to explain to Vanessa that Wen was four years older than I, but that he'd figured out how to keep his stress, and wrinkles, to a minimum. He didn't have children, he'd never been married, and until he'd met me, if he ever felt agitated, he spent a whole day in his hammock, or went skiing in the backcountry for the weekend.

Vanessa had preferred Charlie; she adored him. She went so far as to take his side—inasmuch as there are sides—in the divorce. She thought my ex was a good influence on me, and she found him sensible and generous; they'd agreed on how they felt about me. Wen didn't agree with how other people in my family felt about me.

"An artist and a writer," I'd defended our partnership. "It's a match made in heaven."

"You mean a hedonist and a narcissist," Vanessa had said. "It'll end in tears."

"Let's scatter Dad's ashes when we're next home," I'd suggested.

Vanessa sighed. She had already declared her intention to never come back down to the farm again, or at least for a long, long time; the memorial service had been all the wild heat and chattering ceiling fans she'd needed. Also, four months after Dad's death, his loss was wearing on her; everyone was beginning to annoy and irritate her.

"Well, everyone's bugging me. Even Rich," Vanessa had said.

"Wen is a minister," I'd said.

"No, he's not," she'd said.

"He did it over the internet," I'd said.

Vanessa had sunk back against her pillows, behind her dark glasses, beneath the cats. "Oh, Al-Bo, don't," she'd said. "It's not funny anymore. Bindi says I can't take a single other thing. I have to be left in peace. We should find a proper minister. Dad would have fits."

"No, he wouldn't," I'd said.

"He would." She'd been firm.

"No, he'd never give it a second thought," I'd replied. "Anyway, he liked Wen. They talked about nematodes for hours."

"Well." Vanessa had swallowed a couple of knockout pills from Mum's Indian pharmacist. "Let me state for the record, I'm very angry with you. And I feel very wound up. I am not amused by you, or Wen, or anything about you."

But Mum adored Wen. They stayed up well into the night, long after I'd gone to bed in the guest cottage, Wen riveted by Mum's hilarious and entertaining stories. "She's much wittier than you," he told me. "She's a lot of fun." Wen and Mum agreed that I, on the other hand, was not a lot of fun. I was, they'd concluded, bossy and overbearing.

"Someone has to be," I'd argued.

I'd also given up drinking after Dad died, the better to observe my grief. Mum and Wen had celebrated the coming New Year together in the pub at the bottom of the farm with Boss Shupi and a few of the local dipsomaniac farmers and a couple of fishermen from Lusaka. It was true they shared a joie de vivre that I currently lacked. "I love you," Mum had reportedly told Wen at the stroke of midnight.

"Are you sure?" I'd said after Wen had reported this back to me. "She usually says that to her animals only." But Mum and Wen shared a love of art, also a passionate, immodest love of the dogs; Coco took a special shine to him, she kept stealing his shoes. This amused my mother enormously. Wen had only one pair with him, and they'd been very good shoes, expensive quality; this made my mother even happier. "Coco has very exclusive taste," Mum agreed.

THERE WAS NOTHING IN OUR TRADITION to shove and bump us along in the work of mourning, no ritual or ceremony that declared a lifting or a shift of our sadness. We were like blundering, disconnected, severed children, patching it together the best we could. I leafed through Mum's Book of Common Prayer and drastically shortened the Order for the Burial of the Dead. I was thinking of us standing out there in the heat and humidity, the flies would be thick, and I was also considering the fact that Wen wasn't a minister, really, so the service wouldn't necessarily trip off his tongue.

"We brought nothing into this world, and it is certain we can carry nothing out. The Lord gave, and the Lord hath taken away; blessed be the name of the Lord." It was a reading from 1 Timothy 6:7. I'd shortened the part after the presiding priest says, "Man, that is born of a woman, hath but a short time to live." Also, I'd hacked into the end of the declaration that begins: "Forasmuch as it hath pleased Almighty God of his great mercy to take unto himself the soul of our dear brother here departed."

Since the New Year—I'd made only one resolution—I was try-ing to be less bossy, but organizing the Order for the Burial of the Dead was bringing out my bossiest nature. Also, if I'd been less bossy, Dad would have stayed on Vanessa's bookshelf, perhaps for-ever. It had seemed important that he be laid to rest here sooner rather than later, on the farm, near Mum, under a baobab tree. The narcissism of early grief is blinding: I'd condemned Vanessa's need to wallow, and indulged my propensity to speed; she'd never for-give me for hurrying her along in her grief.

There are three baobab trees at the end of the fishponds. A purple heron perches in the westernmost tree; the egrets roost in the central tree; wild African bees have hived in a hollow of the easternmost tree. It was into this hollow that Mum resolved to put Dad's ashes.

Mum wasn't squeamish. She put her whole hand in the bomb casing while Wen read my drastically edited Order for the Burial of the Dead, and Mrs. Tembo and Mr. Chrissford stood under the hot early-morning sun with silent tears running down their cheeks. I slipped my arm through Nastasya's, and hoped the bees would leave us alone.

"Of course they won't bother us," Mum had said. "Anyway, I'm the only person who's deadly allergic to them." But Mum liked the liveliness of the bees in the tree; the protection they offered the site. "And Dad will overlook everything from here," Mum had said. "It's a very magical, very spiritual spot. It'll terrify everyone."

Baobab trees are iconic: They have smooth metallic-pink heavily folded bark. They're not the tallest of trees, fifty feet or so, but they're sturdy and wide, seventy or eighty feet in diameter. It's said that old baobabs burst into flames by spontaneous combus-tion when they die or become very, very old. Also that a lion would eat anyone foolish enough to pick a blossom from the tree; spirits are supposed to reside in the flowers.

"Yes, it's all very auspicious," Mum had agreed.

She dumped a handful of ashes into a well made by the baobab's enormous roots. The dogs hopped down to investigate. A couple of them returned with white ash on their noses; of course there was the usual leg lifting.

"I think this is probably exactly what Dad didn't want," I said.

"What about this?" Mum asked. She pulled her hand out of the bomb casing and presented for our inspection a piece of dental work; it too was pale grey with ash. "This wasn't Dad's."

"Are you sure?" I asked.

"I'm quite sure," Mum said. "I was always telling him he needed a bridge, but he didn't bother to get his teeth fixed, or his eyes. He said it was like putting new doors on an old pickup, expensive and pointless. And he made such a fuss."

We all stared at the dental work. It was already very hot. The bees were getting restless, they were swarming a bit; I don't know much about African wild bees, but I do know I'd run from them most of my life, especially when their buzzing started to take on an urgent, low hum. "Well, I suppose we should just bury whoever we've been given," I said.

Mum didn't say "I told you so." She didn't need to. She sniffed with all the dignity available to a resilient widow and dug back into the bomb casing for another handful of ashes. "Yes, I suppose we should," she said. She looked solemn. "Whether or not it's poor Dad, or a nameless Hungarian, or an unfortunate"—there was a significant pause—"refugee."

She shook out the last of whoever's ashes they were, minus the bagful Vanessa had reserved for her own private ceremony, onto the roots of the tree. Vanessa said she'd put the rest of Dad in the Zimbabwe highlands, where he'd loved to fish, and until then he'd get plenty of rest on the bookshelf. It was a soothing place, I had to admit, with the Beatrix Potters, the soft Persian cats, the climate control, the perpetually locked door and drawn curtains; not unlike a cozy, homey mausoleum.

The spot under the baobab was less restful; the sun baked down on us pale and yellow, the grass steamed, the fishponds boiled, the dogs hopped about and panted. We all stared at the ashes for a moment, not longer; each of us with our own thoughts of mortality, and thoughts about whose ashes were these, really? Then the bees started to swarm toward the dogs; that shook Mum into action.

"Right, everyone," she said. "Grab a dog, let's get everyone home before the bees lose their patience." She'd been stung by this hive before, when Sarah had come out to stay; her face had swelled up like a soccer ball. "Look at that," she'd said to Sarah at the time, quite thrilled. "Not a single wrinkle. Who knew? Bees are nature's Botox."

THE DEATH OF THE FORCE behind a family is not something the average family of Anglo-Saxon heritage will withstand; Shakespeare knew this, and wrote about it, it's all over the Bible, so perhaps it's a Judeo-Christian trait. The family falls, that's inevitable; but it either falls together or falls apart. That isn't a choice, though; it depends on the family's fault lines.

Also, I don't think you can predict which it is your family will do until it happens, although you might guess, and guess incorrectly that it'll fall one way or the other. And in any case, nothing that happens after death is permanent, not even death—

although it feels that way for a while; or felt that way for me for a while.

"Why can't you and Vanessa just get along and settle Dad's estate?" Mum asked more than a year after Dad had died. Mum and I had always tried to phone each other on Sundays, I in the morning, she in the afternoon. I felt the distance between us most keenly in the Zambian summer, all that lively life chattering through the phone to my deadened Wyoming winter.

"She's not talking to me," I said. "She says Bindi says I am bad for her. She says she is tired of me, and of everything about me."

Vanessa and I had gone through so much, and it's possible we'll go through more, but there's no law or rule that says we have to go through it together, or stay bonded, or loyal every step of the way. In retrospect, it was as if we were sisters who'd stayed together only for the sake of the parents, and now they were half gone, we couldn't hold it together, we couldn't hold it back, we couldn't hold it in. Every untended wound, every ungrieved grievance, a lifetime of unspoken hurt, surfaced. There were terrible rows, and then a terrible silence.

"Well, that's very inconvenient," Mum said.

"Why don't you try speaking to her?" I begged. "Go up to the Rock, and sneak in undercover with a tray of tea."

"I can't imagine what Dad was thinking making you co-executors," Mum said. "I could have told him you'd be at each other's throats."

"But I'm not at her throat," I said. "She's at mine."

"Oh, for heaven's sake," Mum said; she was bored of our performances, I could tell. "I have a very good mind to leave my share of the farm—I am the majority shareholder—to the staff. It's their farm in any case. They do all the work. I won't leave my shares to you or Vanessa. You don't deserve them."

"I think that's a great idea," I said.

There was a long silence on the other end of the phone. I could hear the dogs jostling about. Also, I could hear birds chattering and singing in the background; the North African and European migratory birds would be nesting in the wetlands and garden and all around the fishponds. "Mm," Mum said.

"Don't worry. It'll be all right in the end," I said. "If it isn't all right, it isn't the end."

There was another long pause. "You stole that line from Dad, didn't you?" Mum said.

"Yes," I said. "I did."

"Well, it sounded much more convincing when Dad said it," Mum said. "Much."

CHAPTER FIVE

If You Stay in the Middle of Your Suffering, You'll Never Find the Edge of It

All things considered, I got through childhood relatively unscathed. I'd had the usual: malaria, bilharzia, worms, and a couple of attacks of amebic dysentery. I'd been put through my mother's version of equine therapy. We believed in wearing helmets because we didn't believe in buying calm, expensive horses.

"I hate wimps," Mum said.

She admired people like herself, who were not wimps, and she attributed her own hardiness to the antics of Nane, her Somali pony. He was a little brute with an 8 branded on his haunches; he'd survived lions and the long, grueling trek from Somaliland to Eldoret.

"His early life had tested his patience to the maximum, obviously," Mum said. "I think he hated his life; of course he took it out on me. He would only ever go fast backward, and upward, never forward."

Nane's specialty was slamming on the brakes in the middle of something else, and bucking. He knocked my mother out during morning gallops every day before school; it made it impossible for her to learn to count, but it toughened her up and that mattered more than arithmetic, at least in our lives it did. And in the wholesome, outdoorsy lives of the Huntingfords of Eldoret it had mattered a lot too.

"The nuns complained to my father, 'We can't teach Nicola anything if she's concussed the whole time,' but I learned more from Nane than I ever learned from those resentful nuns at their wretched convent," Mum said.

The unspoken assumption in our family was that easy, pampered, expensive horses led to wimpy children. Difficult, wild, willful ponies gave character to children. I got character from my pony, although he was too poorly coordinated to buck, but he kicked, bit, bolted, and got me off his back every chance he got, every way he could imagine; for a pony he was very creative.

I loved him passionately; I rode daily. I wasn't any good, not like Mum had been. "I was winning races on a much more difficult pony at your age." Mum had nearly despaired. She had a Thoroughbred she'd rescued off the racetrack; he was scarred and had arrived covered in ticks. He wasn't safe to ride either, but he was less creative than my pony.

One morning, my pony scraped me off on a tree and then returned to stomp on me. "He stomped on you?" Mum cross-examined me as best she could after the fact; she sounded like the plodding detective in Agatha Christie's Miss Marple series, unconvinced and certain at the same time. "Are you sure?"

I was fairly sure.

I couldn't move my arms and legs. My head was bashed in; my spine was crushed. It hurt to breathe; it hurt more to talk; it hurt worse to vomit. To take my mind off things until the telephone exchange could reach the family doctor, and until Dad could get down from the cattle dip, Mum tried to get me to see things from the pony's perspective. "I think he was gelded too late," she said. "Maybe he thinks he should have been a stallion. Anyway, Bobo, you'll have to get back on him soon, or he won't think much of you, will he?"

I didn't care what my pony thought of me, but I'd never have let on. "Dismounting without permission," Dad had concurred when he showed up from the cattle dip; Mum had sent a runner from the house. Once a month all the cows were plunged into a toxic bath against ticks and mites and mange. They hated it; it made them bellow. Dad smelled of the toxic dip and cattle, sweat and gun oil. He smoked, waiting for the telephone to ring.

"Cigarette?" he'd offered me. "Or are you trying to give up?"

Mum took the call from the family doctor in the little closet in the corridor where the phone lived; also mice were forever nesting in there, and snakes came after the mice. "She refuses to walk and she's having difficulty talking," Mum yelled into the crackly party line. "You can't get her to shut up normally—and also she says it hurts during breathing."

As if breathing were optional.

"I'm afraid Doc Mitchell says you have to go to the hospital." Mum returned to the bedroom with a long face. "He's spoken to the bone surgeon, and the bone surgeon isn't very chuffed you won't walk." She paused and let me have the really bad news. "Actually, the bone surgeon is furious," Mum said. "He said he doesn't have time for National Velvet in the middle of a war."

"Bad luck, Bobo," Dad said.

There was nothing a Rhodesian child dreaded more than the hospital, except maybe the orphanage. Or to be sent to St. Giles, that would be the worst thing imaginable. St. Giles was the government school in Bulawayo for the Rhodesian reject kids, the cripples and redheads, the kids with hearing aids. I knew a girl at school whose brother had been sent there; it was worse than if he'd died. If I wouldn't walk, I was headed for St. Giles.

It was a measure of the state I was in that I didn't at that moment care. The pain in my back and lungs was off the charts, had anyone been interested in charting my experience. But Rhodesians would never have gone in for smiley faces from saddest to happiest. "Show me your pain," no one would ever have asked. If anything we'd have been shown a chart of grimacing faces from brave to braver to bravest and we'd have been instructed to be manlier.

Except I was a girl, I was ten, and I was in the worst physical pain I'd known until then, although, of course, there'd been grief and terror and other forms of discomfort. "Grit your teeth," Dad advised; he knew all about manliness, the shedding of self it required. "Don't think about it." I gritted my teeth. I tried not to think about it, but I had been reduced, for the first time in my life, to the sum of my biology.

Or my body was a prison of pain from which I couldn't escape.

Afterward, when people had warned me that childbirth was the worst pain I'd ever feel—it's a social contagion upon seeing a pregnant woman, in my experience, to say things like this—I'd kept waiting for it to get as bad as that particular blinding pain, and it was there, but not even close to all the way there.

"Put everything in perspective," Dad always said, unnecessarily really, when Vanessa and I were children. When we were children, everything was already in perspective; war does that, so does suffering, or everyone suffering around you does that, you learn to calibrate. You learn not to draw attention to yourself. "It can always be worse," Dad said, because it could; we could see that for ourselves.

I could endure; Vanessa could endure.

We endured enough.

In the decades since our childhoods, though, something to do with our tolerance for pain became deregulated. Or I'll speak for myself, my own pain. The the-rapists can give it a name or not; the cure's the same for me either way, I'm certain. An untended pain accumulates; pain must be tended, and for it to be tended, it must be endured. But "Pull the plug for anything more than a stubbed toe," I always told my three children. "I'm a horrible patient," I reminded them. "You don't want me lingering."

I didn't want to suffer unnecessarily; that was it, mostly. I'd seen suffering, I'd suffered a little myself; I'd watched what it had taken from people to suffer. It scared me; that, and I hadn't wanted to be a burden to my children. I'd inherited the fear of outstaying my welcome from Dad, the way I'd inherited raucousness from Mum; it was a challenging combination to juggle. Also, it's curious what skips generations, and what shows up in each generation in slightly different forms.

"It's curtains for me, Vanessa," Mum had said grandly as she was wheeled into surgery at the University Teaching Hospital in Lusaka the first time she'd had emergency intestinal surgery. And then, before the doors had slapped shut behind her, in her best brave Memsahib Abroad accent she'd issued her final words to Vanessa and Dad: "Hasta la vista, baby."

Mum hadn't actually watched *Terminator 2: Judgment Day* starring Arnold Schwarzenegger in the title role, but she liked repeating his catchphrase on her deathbed/gurney. It was very Nicola Fuller of Central Africa to get wheeled off into the inner recesses of the teaching hospital's surgical theaters, citing the

Terminator; it had put the wind up everyone. She was behaving terminally in the last place in Zambia that could save your life and therefore where you were very likely to die.

"I cried buckets," Vanessa said afterward. "Mum waved like the queen as they wheeled her off. 'Hasta la whatsit, baby,' she said, and waved. I thought for sure she'd die. That's why I didn't call you. It was awful. Dad got such a fright he nearly ended up in the bed next to hers."

Mum took the blows of her life in the gut, literally. She didn't weep and lament and rend her garments when all was truly lost— her babies dead, three of them, let's start with that—and it wasn't immediately apparent that the unspoken pain of those terrible griefs landed anywhere. But they did, they do. And still Mum will grit her teeth through the pain until she knows the alternative is permanent.

"Those nurses at UTH have seen everything, as you can imagine," Mum said after that first surgery. "It takes quite a lot to shock them." Mum smiled complacently. "But I believe I shocked them to the absolute marrow. 'Madam,' they told me when I could sit up, 'you were a millimeter from death's door.' I was gasping for a cup of tea, who wouldn't be after all that? The doctor said it would kill me; I told him I'd risk it. That impressed the nurses too. They said, 'Ah, madam, you are very strong.'"

Mum's very strong; she's a survivor.

"People say, 'Oh, Nikki, you're a survivor!' as if it's something I enjoy doing, like golf or knitting," Mum told me once. "Or as if it requires no effort to survive; as if I can't help it. But I envy the floppers. I'd love to be able to collapse, and to never have to cope again." She'd sniffed. "Also, I hate it when people call me Nikki. I'm Nicola. Nic-o-la, only three syllables; how much effort can it take to say my whole name?"

Mum can weather and withstand levels of pain and discomfort that have made grown men swoon and that would melt Vanessa and me to a puddle. Vanessa and I had been tough uncomplaining kids. We were not tough uncomplaining adults. Was there only so much each of us could take? Had we become afraid of pain? Had we burned through all our toughness when we were very young?

"I know I did," Vanessa has told me. "It was too much, Al-Bo. Wasn't it?"

"Some of it," I'd agreed.

Or it's what we made of it; and we made too much of it. I made too much of it, I should say. "How many books is it you've written now?" Dad had asked from his deathbed in Budapest.

I'd told him I'd written a few; I'd gone on and on about it, I know. Our lives, I mean; I'd gone through them with a fine-tooth comb and still there were unexpected tangles, whole invisible nests of them. Still there are things I can't know for certain, will never know for certain. Still there are questions to which I will never have an answer.

There are things I can never ask.

All things considered, I don't know how it went for Vanessa; our childhood, I mean. Not because I don't remember. I do, and I've written what I remember. Or because she won't say, she says it was difficult enough. But because getting through a life isn't one thing, it's an accumulation of things, and the weight of a lot of what an adult carries is invisibly left over from other lives. All our lives together we'd been pegs in a spinning wheel and all we'd done is go around; they don't call it cycles of violence for nothing.

I'd asked and probed and made assumptions. I'd turned our stories over and over, seen them in this light and that. I'd asked Vanessa the last question she'd ever entertain.

It's a stalled-out place; to have no questions left.

Or it's the only freedom possible; to have no questions left. To never ask again: Why? Why not? Why bother? Why anything?

We hadn't tended our pain; it had morphed into anger, and back to pain. We were heading toward fifty, but our grief turned us childish; we sulked and bullied and refused to listen to our mother. She advised we do what she'd always done. "I always ignore both of you when you're being impossible," she said. "And then I stop ignoring you when you're being sensible."

"You ignore me all the time," I pointed out.

"Exactly," Mum said.

MUM BANDAGED ME TO A BODY SPLINT; she had first-aid supplies because of being a very serious volunteer of the war effort during our farming-in-a-war-zone phase. I was given a bullet to bite, or I wasn't given a bullet to bite, I wasn't a soldier, merely a civilian; but a convoy was summoned and Dad slid me onto the backseat of our old green Peugeot station wagon. "Let's try to do this with the minimum of fuss," Mum reminded me as we jolted down the uneven driveway and over the culvert at the bottom of the hill where an elderly big black cobra lived. Dad lit another cigarette.

I screamed.

We met the convoy at the top of the valley rim, where the jungle abruptly gave way to the stubble of the Tribal Trust Lands, the overgrazed, overcrowded land allocated to the majority black population under the 1930 Land Apportionment Act. I'd howled; each hairpin turn in the steep road felt as if I were getting skewered. Pain like that is white, and then it's sparkles.

"Huzzit?" Dad had greeted the convoy's commander.

The convoy was small, half a dozen young soldiers in the back of a Land Rover. Their commander was in his twenties, a family friend. Ewan looked as if he'd worked through whatever fright he'd ever had in him long before now; the speed of getting to manhood so fast showed in his jaw. "What've we got here?" he asked, peering into the car. "Bobo, there's a war on. Didn't you hear, girl?"

Dad showed Ewan the FN rifle across his lap; a full magazine locked in, another full magazine between his legs, also the Browning Hi-Power on the seat next to him. Mum showed him her Uzi, a full magazine locked in, a spare at her feet. "I'm very sorry about this," she'd apologized. "Such a fuss."

"Not at all," Ewan said, slapping the side of the Peugeot as if he were the Americans and we were the limping European Allies driving into Vichy France. "Kurumidza!" he shouted to the driver of the Land Rover. That's how we did it; we spoke to one another in Mashona when we'd wanted to emphasize a point. Or we threw a Mashona word in the mix when we wanted to give an order; we were accustomed to the imperative mood. Most of us spoke rotten Mashona, but men like Ewan, if you shut your eyes you couldn't tell the origin of their blood.

Of course that didn't stop us spilling it all over the place.

We had to go through the Tribal Trust Lands to get to the hospital. Naturally the Tribal Trust Lands harbored insurgents. The Rhodesian government had recently issued a warning to the local blacks; "native" children and "native" dogs seen by Rhodesian government forces leaving their kraals would be shot on sight. Meantime, we expected to get shot on sight too, because it was a war; I made a huge fuss over the bumps.

"Try to buck up, Bobo," Mum begged.

I howled and shrieked; I couldn't help it.

Mum grimaced; protesting children put her teeth on edge. She would have put her hands over her ears, except she needed them both to hold the Uzi submachine gun steadily out the window. Also, there was nothing to be done except what was being done. "It doesn't help to holler, Bobo." Mum attempted to be motherly. "Try to think about other cheerful things."

"Hold on, Chookies," Dad said.

"Imagine you're at the seaside," Mum said unhelpfully. I'd never been to any beach except the little bit of sand on the banks of the Nyangombe River in the eastern highlands; it was one of the few bodies of water in which we were allowed to swim because it harbored neither crocodiles nor bilharzia. "Think about a lovely picnic; chocolate cake and éclairs and things," Mum said.

I vomited again.

Clearly I didn't have it in me to suffer the way Mum did; she'd long perfected the art of removing herself from the terrible things that were happening to her, floating off to Mombasa in her head, settling down for a spread of impossible treats. As for Dad, he'd taken the art of suffering a step further; many steps further. "If you stay in the middle of your suffering, you'll never find the edge of it," he said.

I swam for the shores of my agony.

It hurt worse than drowning in it.

Mum and Dad drove into the parking lot of the hospital; it was shaded by jacarandas. The stretcher-bearers whipped me down to the basement of the Umtali General Hospital where the X-ray machines clunked and whirred over the broken bodies of the boys coming back from the front. This wasn't how it was supposed to end, in shreds and tears.

I didn't cry, I knew better; crying made you a waste of white skin. Not crying was supposed to make us whiter, tougher, manlier Rhodesians, less likely to end in shreds and tears, more likely to win the war, eventually. As it was, hardly any of us were up to the challenge. We were more mythical than actual. Or, of course, there were a few white soldiers who were better soldiers than in any other war on the planet and for all time: All wars have those heroes.

I'D LAIN IN THE CHILDREN'S WARD waiting until I would walk again; it wasn't long. But in that time—a couple of weeks at most—I'd become grateful for my crushed spine, my bent ribs, the bulge on my skull; I really didn't have it so bad. I'd felt guilty for taking up room obviously needed for other patients; not that the place was crowded, but the staff were pushed hard.

"If you won't walk, you'll have to lie on a bedpan," the matron had told me. "I can't be hopping in and out all day to take you to the loo."

In the rehabilitation room where I was taken once a day to see if I would walk yet, there were mostly war-shredded boys, eighteen or nineteen years old. They had it worse than I did, much worse. They were headed for St. Giles for sure, some of them, or Ingutsheni Mental Hospital in Bulawayo. In any case, they were done being hard, manly men.

A couple of the boys had bandaged faces, no eyes. They wouldn't see another sunset or another full moon or another msasa forest in full spring colors, orange, red, and lime green. Some of the boys would never do more than sit in wheelchairs for the rest of their lives, like unanswered questions.

They had become unbecoming in one second, a flash of light.

Some of the boys in physical therapy were having a hard time catching up to all the loss they had to absorb. It's not something you can subtract fast enough from yourself, the idea of you gone, in a blink. "Anyone who wants to start a war should have to spend the night in the hospital with the boys who come back from it," Auntie Rena said when she came to visit me in the hospital.

Auntie Rena was the Scottish nurse with cobalt-blue eyes my father was always inviting to Paris. She'd nursed in Aberdeen during the Second World War and in Rhodesia at the start of our war. Now she was our neighbor in a war zone. She bought me a white handbag and a white plastic necklace to wear when I could walk again. "Get back on your feet soon," Auntie Rena wrote in her card.

Mum visited me once too. She bought me a convict's outfit, black-and-white-striped jeans, a black-and-white-striped T-shirt, "For when you escape your imprisonment!" she'd written on her card. She also promised to buy me any shoes I wanted from Bata on the main street, if only I'd walk again.

Dad didn't visit; he'd already said all he had to say. I'd been hurt, I'd get over it, or I'd get used to it. And the sooner I realized it wasn't meant for me, this suffering, the sooner the suffering would end. It wasn't personal; none of it, no suffering was, really.

A bullet didn't really have your name on it, a bee hasn't been informed of your allergy to its sting, ponies have problems of their own to worry about. A mosquito doesn't ask anyone if they feel up to a dose of malaria.

You happened to you, and you took the consequences.

I happened to me, and I took the consequences.

The band struck up and it was correct to turn and face the music. Whatever else you did, you didn't turn the music off. Au contraire. "Music, maestro, music!" I learned from Mum and Dad: You danced through the worst days of your life; and you sat modestly admiring your very good legs on the rare occasions you triumphed. You suffered magnificently.

My parents suffered magnificently.

They'd loved this quality in each other.

Over and over they'd planted a flag on the summit of the highest peaks of their suffering, then they'd slid freely to whatever valley lay below and they made a life there. They faced unthinkable pain not with composure so much, but rather with defiance. A dozen times or more they'd done this, and I come back to this central point again and again; how did they survive it all?

I don't know how they did it, I still don't. In my experience there are certain kinds of pain that go through everything you can do about them. "Love conquers all," people say. But love doesn't conquer all; or sure, perhaps love conquers all in the end, but not immediately. In the short term, a pain so terrible there are no words for it conquers all.

DAD DIED, and Vanessa and I fell apart, separately. Or she went down, and I went down with her; both of us tumbling, our thin skins slicing to ribbons. There were shots in the dark; shots below the belt; shots above the prow.

We sank.

I can see how it happened; from this view, I can see how it was inevitable, the end. We were a whole nation of traumatized children; or the rural kids were; we didn't have sparkling pools and tennis courts like the city kids did, the white city kids, I should say. We performed a childhood gutted of innocence. And the circumstances were what they were.

Bamba zonke, we used to say. Grab it all!

There were no ordinary days; no rests and pauses we could count on. We'd sat down at the table too fast, we'd gobbled too much too quickly. There had been too many lies, too much authority, there had not been enough serenity.

That childhood place was broken, and there's no going back in time to fix it, or to fix us. Vanessa and I were accessories to the fact before we were children. We were squaddies before we were sisters. We were too many things too young to each other, and in the end, or at least in this end, it made all the difference.

Or that's my guess, but I don't know for certain why we fell apart the way we did; and of course there's a chance we'll fall together again just as mysteriously. There's a chance we'll put down our grievances and wounds and stories and stand together around that baobab tree by the fishponds at the last resting place of Tim Fuller the Hon (or of the Nameless Hungarian, or the Unfortunate Refugee) and solemnly feel what it means to be family. Or what it means to be this group of people washed together by blood and marriage and children and love and accident, connected however angrily or briefly or completely or harmoniously, for a time.

If we were all there, it'd be Vanessa and her first husband; it'd be their three boys. And it'd be Rich and the three girls. Also, the grandchildren having children, they'd be there.

It would be my ex-husband and our three children.

It'd be the in-laws we'd accumulated and the extended families, the cousins.

I can't see it happening now, though, not because I have no hope that I will one day be forgiven or at least tolerated and allowed back into our ever-changing family fold, but because the truth is, I can't see beyond now. It was all so fraught after Dad died, and then it got worse. Or worse than that, it got worst. It went to the core of all pains, and beyond my ability to rise above it all.

It went beyond my limited understanding of grief.

The End in the End

This is the way it went, quickly.

I lost Dad, and then in the next two years and three months, everything I'd assumed I'd love forever seemed to tumble after him. I should have known better. Nothing is forever, except forever; Dad had comforted me with this terror my whole life. "If possible, Bobo, try to preserve a bit of energy for the end," he'd said at the end. "You never know when you'll need it."

Maybe he'd seen my end; or maybe all ends are the same.

Vanessa went first after Dad; I mean she removed herself from my orbit, impressively. It takes some doing to break the bonds of a sisterhood like ours, trauma bonds, I mean. Nothing gentle happened in the making of us as sisters; it wasn't a gentle uncoupling. "Hug and make up," a family friend had urged, as if I could walk through walls, and over minefields.

As if I had special powers; or as if Vanessa had a magic wand.

Vanessa's superpower is her downfall; she can see into my future. My superpower is my downfall; I can see into my future too. We both argued about who could see more clearly, more correctly. We both lied about the superiority of our visions.

Although it turned out, I couldn't see into the future. I could dimly see only the present, and because of this, I could see how it would end. It was as if our past had dipped a toe into the puddle of now, and stirred up the water, muddying everything with what had been left undone, unspoken, unfelt, untouched. "Are we in the same decade?" I'd asked Vanessa, trying to catch up.

But she really wasn't speaking to me by then. Vanessa wasn't speaking to Wen either. She'd hated my passion for him. I'd loved him like I'd never loved anyone; he'd reached a whole chamber of my heart I hadn't known.

I'd been delirious with love; certain of love; convinced of love.

We'd moved into a yurt together the year Dad died, Wen and I. We tore down his old yurt; we'd bought a new one and furnished it with a proper stove, a stand-up fridge. "This is my dream," Wen had told me. He'd put the yurt up, friends had helped; we'd planned to live in it forever, partners and co-conspirators. I'd loved the way the yurt felt like the house on the farm without the snakes, without all the uncertainty.

I'd seen them from the road in the two decades I'd lived in this western Wyoming valley, this flotilla of yurts out in the middle of the sagebrush in an old agricultural campground, overlooked by mountains and prayer flags. I'd wondered about the place; it seemed to me that once you were antisocial enough to live in a yurt park with a shared ablution block, you were probably too antisocial for communal living. Or maybe it would be like a village in Zambia, and there'd be all the usual backbiting, and someone would always be threatening to shove someone headfirst down the communal latrine, but it'd be a noisy, lively community. You'd never feel alone.

Wen had taken me to his yurt on our first date, and I'd fallen for it all—for him, for the place, for the idea of us—so completely I hadn't really ever left. It was like camping, or being in the bush; the elements were in the yurt, around us, the sky an endless shimmering show. I was smitten with it all.

"You'll hate it," Mum had said. "You're intolerant and bossy in small spaces."

"I'll love it," I'd said. "It'll be like boarding school, but without the rules."

"There's a way to move around a yurt meditatively," Wen had told me, then he'd instructed me, and finally he'd begged; I moved like a tornado. He didn't meditate, but he had meditated, and he liked it when other people meditated; he liked Buddhists and monks. He'd have preferred me with less energy, less grief and drama certainly.

We'd put up the new yurt on old fault lines, Wen and I, of course we had. There's only so much any structure can absorb; we hadn't accounted for my grief. I was so much; it was all too much. The insomnia, the weeping, the unaccountable rage that accompanies intense grief, the nights in front of the Fisher stove while a long Wyoming winter crackled outside, wolves howling; a yurt's a small space. "I need more room for my own thoughts," Wen had begged.

Cycles of grief scoured and scoured.

I bought a sheep wagon, a covered wagon with a bed and a small stove and I put it next to the yurt. I moved my grief and my early-morning writing in there, and still it wasn't enough room for Wen to have a thought of his own. Finally, he'd had enough, he'd made it clear, for all these reasons, and more reasons.

Words are unstable and inadequate in any end.

I fled. I took what I could carry. There'd never been a partnership, it turned out. Or if there'd been a partnership, we tore it to pieces as if all that love had happened to other people in another time. Also, there'd been more anger than I'd expected. I'd cost Wen, he told me. My love had taken a heavy emotional toll on him. He'd been unable to work when he'd been with me.

"Know when to cut your losses," Dad had always said.

But the end of Wen and me hadn't felt merely like losses; it felt like the end, or at least the end of hope and love and youth. I'd expected to let those things go, just not now, all at once. This love had been, I'd thought, my last and lasting love, and cutting it had been so final, so brutal, so difficult to do; all that vanity and wounding that accompanies the end of love.

Still, it wasn't something my children needed to see, my ruined relationship strewn across their lives. I tried to make it look less messy, more seamless, as if I were jumping not falling, flying not flailing. "You're a survivor," Wen wrote to me after I'd taken refuge with friends. We'd gone from love to this scoured wreckage in the same time it had taken us, in reverse, to fall in love. We couldn't see each other; it was like we'd been shaken apart in an earthquake.

I BELIEVED THIS to be the greatest sadness of my life: My father's death, my sister's anger, my family's silence, the end to the yurt, the end of my engagement to Wen, the end to the arrogance of my certainty, it all hurt. My father had been dead two and half years, and my life appeared to be racing away from me.

Dad had not left me with instructions for this; he'd loved my mother truly, without the need to possess her, or even to have her love in return. I'd said it and said it and said it to Wen and that had been my mistake, or one of my mistakes. Love isn't a word, it's a whole life.

I'd loved him so much I believed him to be the cure for my soul; and because of this, he was. We'd slept together under that yurt's plexiglass dome, the sky skidding toward dawn above our heads, the dog sleeping at our feet, my youngest child asleep in a loft above our heads.

In my grief, I'd never been so happy.

But grief puts you to sleep for a hundred years; or pain blunts your awareness. Something happens when you lose too much too fast; you stop tracking. Dad died and I couldn't write like I had; the old thoughts wouldn't come, my words were bitter and angry and godforsaken. Then Wen and I ended, and it was as if unseen hands had pushed me down an icy slope, a slippery slide. I had to write; words were my self-arrest in every way. "I will write my way out of this"—I'd had that sign above my computer before. I wrote it out again, pinned it up above my desk.

I woke up at four to write. "No, it's fine," I lied to the kids. "I will be okay." Fuller was in Argentina, his semester abroad. Sarah was writing for the local paper. Cecily was sailing through her first year of middle school. They hadn't been as attached to Wen as I, obviously. "It's for the best," I pretended.

When you're all the way down to the bone, Dad had said.

I patched together a routine so that Cecily wouldn't notice a disruption to her schedule. Friends let me sleep on their floors and sofas and in their spare rooms; they gave me whole houses to live in. Dad would have said how lucky I was, but I kept thinking of my losses, my incomprehensible losses, I counted them all day and night. I carried them with me like millstones.

THAT SPRING WAS the saddest of my life.

How I longed for Wen, all the way into the start of a hot

summer. Aries rising red and early in the east, dominating the skyline. I remember that; and trying to fall in love again too soon, I remember that. All through the noise of the breakup and the breakup's aftermath I'd longed for Wen, and for solitude. I remember the moons of those months holding me; they were fat and silver.

I'd wept and wept, each moon.

Then Fuller had had a seizure in Argentina; he'd awoken to find himself in the ICU. Charlie, my ex-husband, and I bought air tickets the day of the incident. It was decided I would stay with our youngest and see her through the beginning of her summer holidays; he'd fly down. Fuller came home with him. He'd been funny and brave, Fuller, waking up in the emergency room in a strange country; no one speaking his language. "I'm literally naked and afraid," he'd joked to me on the phone.

Oh, perspective!

"Just come home in one piece," I'd begged.

He did; he'd been checked out at our local hospital, deemed fine. A week later, he died in his sleep. I knew he'd died the moment I saw the text from Charlie flash up on my phone, "Call me." I knew then what had happened, because all parents carry that fear somewhere in their cells; my body knew before my ears would hear the words, our son had died.

Daughter of a ghost.

Mother of an ancestor.

The son is dead. The sun would never rise again. Days would drag themselves from nights, but the sun wouldn't erupt from the horizon and blaze a new day open.

I wouldn't know warmth again.

Son, brother, grandson, activist, friend, scholar, athlete, reader, thinker, lover, and all of this by twenty-one; oh, my prodigious boy, where are you going so fast without your mother? We'd read poems about this when he was little, and books.

I had anticipated an apocalypse in our lifetime, at this rate. I had prepared the children for that; the dogs eating bloated bodies in the streets. But I hadn't prepared my children, or myself, for this; that's a cruelty beyond words.

Apocalypse, from the Greek *apokalupsis, apokaluptein,* to reveal things as they really are; everything was revealed, all my anger, my denial, my bargaining, my habits and practices and witchcraft and love.

My love deeper than any ocean, I'd told him.

Limitless, to the sky and moon and other universes beyond imagination, my love.

My love more than myself, of course more than myself.

Fuller died free, in his own bed. He'd died painlessly, without foreknowledge. His father had been the first to find him; that's a dark privilege not often granted. He'd lived twenty-one full years, without undue harassment.

He'd been lucky, and we'd been lucky too.

But you can't tell yourself what your mind refuses to believe.

I knew the sound that was coming from my mouth as I ran toward his; I recognized the pleading. How I would come to know the sound of a wolf howling, the baying of my sorrow. It was the sound of every mother separated from every child for all time and in all places. It was the sound my own life made as it came out of my mouth.

I went with him, naturally, to his death.

I'd made that promise to him at his birth. "I'll love you forever, and in all ways," I'd told him over and over. "I'll always be there, always." He'd been a gentle son, the easiest child, the beloved middle; he was a given, a certainty. "A keeper," my ex-father-in-law had observed at the time, by which he'd meant *male issue, thank God.*

Cycles can be invisible; they can overlap.

Charlie had wanted to name our son for himself, for his family, for my father, and for our family. I can see now, it's an inheritor's thing to do, three names on one child, straddling all those generations and continents. Charles Fuller Ross, but we called him Fuller. "Fi," he'd named himself when he was too little to wrap his mouth around the difficulty of his name. Fi, I'd called him after that, it had suited him.

Semper Fi.

I know this now.

When he died, there was an immediate pain so terrible, it had no color; it went beyond white, beyond sparkles. And even then, as that pain swept over me, I knew it wasn't the real pain; it was only the shock before the real pain. I knew too, my pain would be the precise size of the love I had for my son; it would have no end, it would have no shape, it would shape me.

I'd become it; I'd have to learn to cope with it, to face this difficult music, and dance. "Fi," I told him, collapsing next to his body, my fingers going to the bruises on his face from the seizure, oh the instinct to remove pain is eternal. "I'm here." How terrible; the impossibility of time, plodding over us, unstoppable, dreadful thieving. I no longer needed to imagine grief upon grief. And still I couldn't comprehend how a body can withstand losing so much at once, and more with each step.

What grief.

I've thought since then, but I haven't done this *alone*. Friends flocked and descended. Friends surrounded me, moved for me. They held me and breathed for me.

I'm grieving one good son once.

I'm not being forced to break stone while grieving; or to fear my own death; or to fear the death of my daughters, although I do, or wonder incessantly of their whereabouts, although I do. And still you can't begin to believe the power of a mother's grief, I couldn't believe it, it staggered me, myself.

You can't imagine the drenching of tears, for a start. Or you can, but you'd never go inside the agony of it unforced, it's too much. It's why every thoughtless violent thing has ever happened, because none of us want to imagine parents grieving children, over and over.

What love; love upon love.

I ran my fingers through Fi's auburn hair, breathed in the last of his scent; how I'd loved this boy, how he'd loved life. "I love you. Forgive me. Thank you." Over and over I said the words to his impossibly still body; so perfect, so young and strong and necessary. At last, by evening, the coroner insisted, the police insisted, the doctors insisted, he be taken.

And then we'd held our two daughters, Charlie and I.

Oh, our inconsolable souls.

Fi died under a waning crescent moon two years, ten months, and four days after my father had died under a blood moon. I befriended that moon; I stare into her face, nightly I implore her, "Take me with you, somehow."

And yet leave me too; spare me, for my daughters, until they're able to dispense of a mother.

Tear me to pieces, please, and spread me among my children.

Bury me with my boy; please, dear God, fall upon us from above, and bury us all.

———

WHEN YOU'RE ALL THE WAY down to the bone, Dad had said.

Maybe he'd seen this moment, or moments like it; the end of the world is the end of the world, after all. He'd been here himself; his family had banished him from their lives, he'd taken his children to the grave without them, he'd buried his son with his own hands in the cemetery in Salisbury.

There was nothing to be done, except what was being done.

Friends moved me into a condo, they painted it, fixed shelves in rooms, hung curtains, fixed drywall and windows. There'd been drug addicts in the condo before I'd moved in. The neighbors wondered if I too were a drug addict, the noise for a start. The people coming and going all hours, with casserole dishes?

My friends brought meals, and poured me baths. They did laundry, and made gallons of South African tea for me. I cried for my mother, any mother, and for my sister, any sister. I roared and roared into the dark for my son, and when the silence of his nonreply grew deafening, I howled in protest. I missed Wen. My friends slept on the floor, they took turns passing out on my sofa; friends lay on the bath mat while I wept and wept in the tub. Friends crawled into bed, one on each side of me, and held me.

My logical blood never left me; I never left me, although the impulse was strong.

And I grieved bodily. I grieved the space where, in my mind's calculation, Vanessa should be and Mum should be and Wen should be. Most of all I grieved the space where my son should be. The basic aggression of wanting things to be different is separation from God; by another name, it's hell, but you can't always see it when you're in it. For a start, it's a long way down.

I made a bed on the porch, and Sarah nested there; she didn't sleep, she scanned the world restlessly for her beloved brother.

Her grief was terrible to witness. But then she started to write, and watching her take the impossible step from a life *in* death to a life *with* death, I started to write too. We got up. We got up and paid attention to the sisters and mothers and families whose loss was more senseless than ours, and learned from them how to grieve fruitfully.

We got up at four.

We rescued a puppy for Cecily; I'd learned some indelible lessons from Mum. "Moss," Cecily named him, smitten. "Do you think Fi sent him?"

Moss is white with a black heart-shape on his face; he has big puppy paws and hazel eyes. At four months, he flops across our laps like overcooked linguine, he drapes himself on the bed in the best position for a tummy rub; he knows nothing of our grief.

"I'm almost certain Fi did," I said.

Two months after Fi died, I dragged the sheep wagon out to the Wind River Mountains and parked it beside a brook overhung with pine trees; there were cliffs that reminded me of Zimbabwean kopjes, you'd expect a leopard to come out of the shadows, but it doesn't. I build a fire in the little stove, keep it going most of the day, and every day I do the same thing; I sit in silence at the foot of the mountains until I am no longer there.

Or I am everywhere, in all things, dissolved in my own salty tears; worn out by my yearning. I am nothing, and everything; I am the wind, and the water, the fire, the metal. Fi is those things too. For the hours and hours each day I am still, observing every creak, aware of each breath, I can feel whole again, almost; or the wrenching apartness is less terrifying when I know the result is that I'm becoming him in my silence.

I'm becoming him, my beloved dead; I listen for him always.

And in an effort to hear him, I forgive and forgive; grief makes a miser of your emotions, it makes of you the most attentive listener, it makes of you a supplicant. In the end, grief makes of you its humble servant.

Take everything of me, for one glimpse of him.

I have no room for anything else. I can't see my daughters, I can't see myself. I've disappeared, I am disappearing; I am eaten up by grief. The weight slides off my bones. My love for this dead boy threatens to swallow me completely until one day I allow it to, and on that day I can say the words out loud, "Fi is dead."

I am nowhere now, and it's a start.

When you're lost, go downhill until you find a river.

I'd seen that text; opened the car door and run downhill, lost. There's no easy way to get comfortable with being lost, loss. How my father had done it, I think I know, but God knows where he'd found the strength.

When I come home from the Wind River Mountains, wind-burned, sunburned, tattered, I put a note on the door to remind the girls and myself to put one foot in front of the other anyway. Our footsteps are lonely, singular; they are without voices, like the sound of pigeon wings, or like fat raindrops on a tin roof.

But we'll laugh again, I believe.

We'll be okay.

We won't always be in pain beyond color. One day, none of us will have cried for him. You can survive more than you'd believe; Dad had told me that. He'd also told me you can survive more than you want; but it's not always up to you, not the enormous things, those are beyond all control.

"Hold on, Chookies," Dad would have said, my life in tatters and tears. "It'll be all right in the end."

And if it's not all right, it's not the end.

I no longer pretend to know what the end may look like, and I've lost the arrogance to take a guess. Nor do I have the energy to keep entertaining myself with possibilities and impossibilities of what the end is, but I know the end is not now.

Or it is an end; all ends.

And therefore, I can only assume it's also a beginning; all beginnings.